BUDGET
Horse & Pony Care

BUDGET
Horse & Pony Care

Cost Effective Horse Management

Tamsin Pickeral

Kenilworth Press

First published in the UK in 2009
by Kenilworth Press, an imprint of Quiller Publishing Ltd

British Library Cataloguing-in-Publication Data
A catalogue record for this book
is available from the British Library

ISBN 978 1 905693 29 0

Edited by Martin Diggle
Designed and typeset by Paul Saunders
Photographs and diagrams by the author

Printed in China

Kenilworth Press

An imprint of Quiller Publishing Ltd
Wykey House, Wykey, Shrewsbury, SY4 1JA
Tel: 01939 261616 Fax: 01939 261606
E-mail: info@quillerbooks.com
Website: www.kenilworthpress.co.uk

Contents

Measurements and terms

Measurements throughout this book are given in both imperial and metric. Regarding liquid measure, please note that where 'pint' is used, this refers to the UK measure of 20 fl oz (0.568 litre), whereas the US pint is 16 fl oz (0.473 litre).

Introduction

Horses *can* be expensive creatures, and riding them is a pursuit that *can* make money disappear faster than a rabbit down a hole. It is inevitably not the cost of buying the horse (or even the lessons on school horses) that has the most alarming effect on the bank balance, but instead the cost of maintenance, feed, farriers, vets, accessories, tack, trailers, vehicles, competition entries, clothing (equine and human) and the 'add on' cats and dogs that seem to accumulate around yards – that also demand to be fed and tended.

Mounting expenses can seem daunting, and money is easily spent, particularly on the 'fashionable' items that have become so popular in recent years. Once, a rug was a rug, was a rug, and it came in brown or brown; now the choice in every area of the industry is at times overwhelming, with products simply screaming out to be bought. At most risk, of course, are indulgent parents whose children are inexplicably mesmerised by what appear to be an increasing number of pink horse accessories – though children are not alone in being drawn in by sparkling browbands and elegant personalised equipment.

Nevertheless, there *are* ways that money can be saved around horses – although it must be stressed that economy measures should never be at the expense of the horse's welfare or safety. *Budget Horse and Pony Care* presents a number of ways in which the horse owner or rider can cut down on their costs, with these effectively falling into two categories; making one's own products and equipment, and considering stable/yard practices designed to economise. In both categories, as an important unifying theme, a balanced 'green' approach to horse products, care and maintenance is encouraged.

First, the book addresses a selection of equine products that can be made quite easily at home more cheaply than buying them commercially. In particular, products such as shampoo and other grooming or first aid products and liniments are economical, quick and easy to make, with the added advantage that one can use wholesome, 'green' ingredients. There are instances where it is not always cost-effective or indeed simple to make one's own products – items such as waterproof rugs being an example – and these are pointed out. There are also occasions when making one's own equipment, although time-consuming, can be greatly rewarding, and the reader is encouraged to weigh the cost of their own time against the cost of purchasing the product. Often, simply overhauling existing products, such as applying logos or initials to rugs, changing buttons on jackets or 'blinging-up' browbands, is sufficient to give the item a fashionable new look, whilst making items of equipment such as rugs, travelling gear and even show jumps from scratch, with easy-to-follow instruction, is also discussed. Additional to the many instructions and recipes for making things there are also numerous tips, particularly on show turnout and grooming, tack care and first aid matters.

The second aim of the book is to encourage the horse/yard owner to take stock of their stable and yard routine, to consider ways to economise, and to keep the stable environment as natural and eco-friendly as possible. There are instances when stable yards have the potential to increase their revenue, and *Budget Horse and Pony Care* covers various different ideas that could work in different situations, as well as discussing the conversion of existing buildings into stables, and the important factors that must be considered when doing so. Feeding, bedding and pasture management are all areas where the responsible horse person can take stock and save money through sensible stable management practices. For example, although the *quality* of all feeds should never be compromised, and only the best should be fed, there are still ways to economise, namely cutting down on waste through poor storage, only buying in what is eaten within a two-week period and checking brand names and ingredients against each other. There are instances (and this applies to some feed supplements as well) when lesser-known brands contain exactly the same ingredients and nutrient levels as their significantly more expensive and better known alternatives.

Thus *Budget Horse and Pony Care* provides much fodder for thought, and is packed full with good ideas, instructions, recipes, old-fashioned tricks and tips, and different ways of considering the approach to horse care and management.

CHAPTER 1

Looking good

Looking good is hard work for a horse – even one born with the face of an Arab and the body of a Thoroughbred. Even the best-looking equines have their bad hair days! Looking good in essence stems from being healthy and happy. The horse's health and well-being are paramount, and when these aspects are neglected this is quickly manifest through the quality of the coat, alongside the animal's general demeanour. If the horse's coat appears excessively dull, staring, greasy, scurfy or brittle there is cause for concern, and the cause, which could be diet-related, or a general health problem should be investigated. That said, every horse is different and some horses are prone to scurf (US dander), while others may exhibit a drier quality that particularly shows up in the mane and tail. Very dry climates will affect the quality of the mane and tail, and strong sunlight will bleach and lighten a dark coat.

Some horses naturally have a thicker mane or tail than others, and while there are expensive products that can be used on the mane and tail that are claimed to thicken them up, essentially the abundance of mane and tail growth comes down to simple genetics. Providing the horse with a balanced nutritional intake is the primary way to ensure the quality (as opposed to quantity or thickness) of coat, mane and tail. Some horses suffer from poor and brittle feet (often in these instances the coat will also lack lustre) and a supplement, which should contain biotin, methionine and lysine can be helpful in improving their quality – which again is reflected in an improvement in the coat, mane and tail.

Tip

To prevent a dark coat being bleached by sunlight, turn the horse out in a UV ray repellent fly sheet, or use fly spray with an anti-UV ray factor in it, or turn out at night when it is cooler and keep stabled during the day.

Treatments for manes and tails

Shampoos and conditioners

One of the key elements when making your own items is the ease with which they can be made. Most people fight the clock and so the simplest and least time-consuming products tend to have the greatest appeal. Making shampoo and conditioners can be very simple and economical, and affords one the opportunity to add exactly what is needed. Homemade shampoos and conditioners do not have a sudding agent added, so they will produce less lather. This does not mean they are not working! Also they are often not as thick or regular in consistency as commercial products, but again this does not detract from their effectiveness.

How to make shampoo

There are many different recipes for homemade shampoo, but a good basic recipe, to which other ingredients may be added, is as follows.

Basic shampoo
2 pints (1.14 litres) of water
4 oz (114 grams) soap flakes (these can be bought extremely cheaply from any supermarket and are found in the washing detergent aisle)

Bring the water to the boil and pour over the soap flakes stirring continuously until they have completely dissolved. This makes the base for the shampoo, and various essential oils can then be added to make the shampoo more specific.

Lavender shampoo – soothing, anti-itch
2 pints (1.14 litres) of water
4 oz (114 grams) soap flakes
2 tsp (10 ml) of surgical spirit (US rubbing alcohol)
8–10 drops of lavender oil

Prepare the basic shampoo using the boiling water and soap flakes. Dissolve the lavender thoroughly in the surgical spirit and add to the shampoo mix. Stir thoroughly and allow to cool before pouring into a recycled plastic or glass bottle. Don't forget to label the bottle! This lavender shampoo is very calming and is good for horses that have an irritable skin, are itchy, have scurf have or are prone to insect bites.

Tip

Dri Pak soap flakes are very good. They are cheap to buy and are free from any additives, perfume, bleach, enzymes or phosphates, plus their packaging is made from recycled materials.

The ingredients for making shampoo and conditioner are readily available.

Peppermint shampoo – invigorating, anti-insect

2 pints (1.14 litres) of water

4 oz (114 grams) soap flakes

2 tsp (10 ml) of surgical spirit (US rubbing alcohol)

8–10 drops of peppermint oil

Prepare the ingredients as described above. The peppermint is an invigorating oil, and can be combined with lavender and rosemary (4–6 drops of each) to make a refreshing and stimulating shampoo, that also has insect repelling properties. For a similarly invigorating effect the peppermint can be replaced with 8–10 drops of lemon or citrus oil.

A word on essential oils

These can be expensive to buy initially, but are only ever used in tiny amounts, so last for a long time. Essential oils are extremely potent in their distilled form and should not be used indiscriminately; always follow the instructions, or seek advice. Prices for essential oils also vary quite significantly. Price-check using the internet but remember to factor in the cost of postage and packaging. Sometimes it is cheaper to purchase them in the shop.

Camomile and peppermint shampoo – soothing, anti-insect

6 camomile teabags

1½ pints (0.85 litre) of water

4 tbsp (60 ml) soap flakes

1½ tbsp (22 ml) glycerine

1 tsp (15 ml) surgical spirit (US rubbing alcohol)

8 drops of peppermint oil

1 tbsp coconut oil

Steep the teabags in the boiling water for 20 minutes, then squeeze out the bags and discard. Mix the soap flakes in the tea, and stir in the glycerine and coconut oil. Make sure the ingredients are completely dissolved and mixed together. Dissolve the peppermint oil in the surgical spirit and add to the shampoo, mixing thoroughly. When cool enough pour into a recycled bottle and store in a cool, dark place. This shampoo has a tendency to settle out, so shake the bottle really well before use, also try to make up what you will use: because there are no preservatives in the mix it will not last very long and should be used within a month. The coconut oil helps the shampoo to lather, and is also good for dry skin. It can be bought from most health food shops.

Anti-scurf shampoo

1 pint (0.57 litre) water

2 oz (57 grams) soap flakes

2 tbsp (30 ml) apple cider vinegar

6 tbsp (90 ml) apple juice

1 tsp (5 ml) rum extract

8 finely ground cloves

Prepare the base shampoo by mixing the soap flakes in the boiling water, then stir in the vinegar, apple juice and rum extract. Grind up the cloves until they are almost powdered (use a blender) and add this to the mix. This shampoo is very good for lifting scurf and dandruff and leaves the coat really shiny.

Shampoo for greasy coats

2 pints (1.14 litres) of water

4 oz (114 grams) soap flakes

2 tsp (10 ml) surgical spirit (US rubbing alcohol)

10 drops rosemary essential oil (peppermint can also be used)

10 drops lemon essential oil

8 drops lavender essential oil

Tip

Rosemary is also good for dark coats and helps to keep them lustrous and shiny. Lemon is good for paler coats and has a highlighting effect (particularly good for flaxen manes and tails).

Mix the base shampoo as described above and dissolve the essential oils in the surgical spirit before adding to the mixture. Be sure to mix up well, then allow to cool and pour into a recycled bottle.

Shampoo for dry coats

2 pints (1.14 litres) of water
4 oz (114 grams) soap flakes
4 tbsp (60 ml) of olive or almond oil
1½ tbsp (22 ml) glycerine
1 tsp (5 ml) surgical spirit (US rubbing alcohol)
10 drops of lavender oil
1 tbsp (15 ml) coconut oil

Mix up the base shampoo and add the olive or almond oil, glycerine and coconut oil, stirring well to ensure all ingredients mix. Dissolve the lavender oil in the surgical spirit and add to the mix. Allow to cool and pour into a recycled bottle.

Tip

Allow shampoo mixes to cool before pouring them into their containers, especially if these are recycled plastic. However do not allow them to cool and set, otherwise they are hard to pour.

Some basic essential oils that can be used in shampoo

Chamomile – soothing
Cedarwood – combine with rosemary for anti-dandruff, good for greasy coats
Eucalyptus – insect repellent and antiseptic properties
Ginger – stimulant
Jasmine – good for dry skin, combines well with chamomile and rose
Lavender – soothing, good for skin problems
Lemon – stimulant and bleaching qualities
Patchouli – combines well with lavender, good for dry skin
Peppermint – stimulant, refreshing, anti-insect
Rose – soothing, good for dry skin, combines with lavender
Rosemary – stimulant, good for oily skin
Sandalwood – good for dry skin
Tea tree – insect repellent, good for dandruff, *do not combine with other oils*

Essential oils not suitable for sensitive skin

Basil	Clove
Bergamot	Ginger
Black pepper	Tea tree
Cedar	

How to make conditioner

Like the shampoos, there are a number of recipes for making conditioners. These recipes involve perishable ingredients such as mayonnaise, avocado and egg. Obviously, when making conditioners using these ingredients only make up what will be used because they will not last! These conditioners are most suitable for use on the mane and tail. The body hair should not need a wash in/wash out conditioner; instead use one of several rinses, listed under How to Make Rinses later this chapter.

Quick and easy conditioner
4 tbsp (60 ml) mayonnaise
1 avocado
4 tbsp (60 ml) olive or almond oil

De-stone and mash the avocado and mix with the mayonnaise and oil. Taking a small amount at a time, massage into the mane and crest, and the tail. If your horse will tolerate it, wrap the neck and also the tail in cling film (Saran wrap US) and leave for 20 minutes to work its magic. Wash off thoroughly.

Deep conditioner
1 avocado
4 tbsp (60 ml) olive oil
4 tbsp (60 ml) almond oil
4 tbsp (60 ml) coconut oil
4 tbsp (60 ml) honey
4 tbsp (60 ml) vegetable shortening

De-stone and remove the avocado from its skin and combine with the other ingredients and heat over a low heat, stirring constantly. Remove from the heat and allow to cool until the mixture is lukewarm. Massage into the mane and tail, cover with cling film (Saran wrap) if the horse will tolerate it, and leave for 20 minutes. Wash off thoroughly.

Egg conditioner
1 avocado
2 egg yolks
4 tbsp (60 ml) olive or almond oil

De-stone and mash the avocado, then add the egg yolk and oil and mix thoroughly (a blender works well). Massage into the mane and tail and leave for 20 minutes before washing off.

Leave-in conditioner

There are lots of leave-in conditioners on the market, some of which are much better than others, but all of which are expensive! They are an essential element of the grooming kit and work in two related ways. First, they should keep the hair quality soft and in good condition, and second, by keeping the hair in good shape, they should make combing through and removing tangles easier, with less likelihood of breaking off the hairs.

Basic leave-in conditioner
2 pints (1.14 litres) of water
2 tbsp (30 ml) of baby oil
1 tbsp (15 ml) of Listerine original

Mix the ingredients well and keep in a clearly labelled spray bottle – it is that simple.

The trick is not to use too much baby oil in the mixture. If it becomes too oily then the conditioner will make the hair greasy and will attract dust and dirt. The Listerine helps to combat scurf and itchiness. For horses that are really itchy, double the Listerine to 2 tbsp (30 ml) per 2 pints (1.14 litres) of water.

Alternative leave-in conditioner
2 tbsp (30 ml) rosewater and glycerine
1 pint (0.57 litre) of water
½ pint (0.28 litre) of white vinegar

Mix the ingredients in a spray bottle and apply liberally. This keeps the coat soft and shiny and also helps to repel flies.

Almond hair shine
2 pints (1.14 litres) of water
4 tsp (20 ml) lemon juice
10 drops almond oil
1 tsp (5 ml) cherry extract
1tsp (5 ml) vanilla essence

Combine all the ingredients, mix well and store in a labelled spray bottle. This conditioner does not need to be rinsed off and leaves the coat really shiny (it smells good, too).

De-tangling

To de-tangle really stubborn knots or to remove sticky berries or burrs a handful of straight baby oil applied to the problem area can help, although it should be shampooed afterwards. Similarly WD40 sprayed (always take care when using aerosol products on the horse as many horses will react to the noise) onto the problem area can be useful in removing serious tangles. Always wash out immediately afterwards with soap and water. Most shop-bought leave-in hair conditioners and de-tanglers contain silicon, and it is this that makes the hair feel so instantly smooth and helps to untangle knots. WD40 acts in a similar way, although it should not be used regularly.

Another way to de-tangle a seriously matted mane or tail is to wash it using the shampoo for dry hair (see earlier this chapter) and then rinse it with warm water containing a capful of fabric softener. Only use this on the ends of the tail and not on the dock area. Use a non-biological eco-friendly softener, and always patch test to make sure the horse is not allergic to it.

A word on brushes and combs

Equine brushes can be expensive. Use an old human hairbrush instead, the ones that are cushioned are the best and the gentlest on the hair; avoid the stiff nylon variety.

Avoid over-brushing the mane and tail as this breaks the fragile hairs off; try to use your fingers to de-tangle and tease out the hair instead. Always start brushing from the bottom of the hairs and work your way up, and apply leave-in conditioner (see later in this chapter) before starting to brush. Mane combs – the metal variety – are essential for pulling manes, and cannot be substituted, but are generally cheap to buy. Plastic human combs, especially those with a pointed end, can be very useful for plaiting manes and tails, using the pointed end to divide up the sections of hair. These are generally very cheap to buy. Cheap plastic combs are also useful for creating quarter markings (without using a template), and are a useful addition to the grooming kit. A great place for sourcing cheap grooming tools is the Pound Shop; almost every large town has one! Generally they have on sale all manners of combs, brushes, sponges, boxes, spray bottles and even occasionally shampoos and gels, all massively discounted.

Manes

The mane should be encouraged to lie on the correct side, which is the off side (right). Do this by damping a brush and brushing the hair over to the right side daily. It can also be helpful to divide the mane up into bunches or plaits and securing these with bands to train the hair to grow over, but never leave plaits in for longer than 12 hours. The mane should be thoroughly washed to remove scurf and to keep it silky and smooth. The frequency with which the mane should be washed is based on common sense; some horses are naturally cleaner, less scurfy and will have a less greasy mane and coat than others. There are a number of equine shampoos and condition-

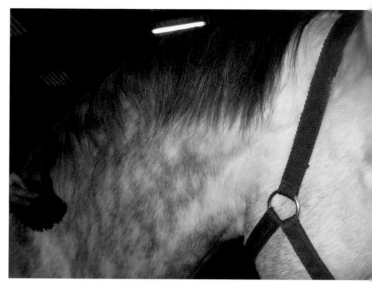

Encourage the mane to lie flat by dampening it.

ers on the market, but as described earlier it is easy to make your own, which are much cheaper and 'greener' than commercial brands. If preparing the horse for a competition, be sure to wash the mane at least four days prior to the event, otherwise the hair will be too smooth and slippery, making plaiting-up difficult. The use of a leave-in mane conditioner (see How to Make Conditioner, earlier this chapter), is a good way of keeping the quality of the hair soft and tangle free.

Keeping manes tidy

Bridle paths

Keeping the bridle path closely trimmed, preferably with clippers (although scissors will work), greatly effects the overall look of the neck and head. When trimming the bridle path take care not to take off any of the forelock; stop trimming approximately one finger's width behind the ears (avoid trimming forward between the ears). The bridle path should be approximately 1 in (2.5 cm) for horses being ridden English style, 4–5 in (10–12.5 cm) for Quarter Horses being ridden in Western disciplines, and 6–8 in (15–20 cm) for Arabs. Also keep the bottom end of the mane that straggles onto the withers, neatly trimmed away. This gives the bottom of the neck a better definition and stops wispy bits of mane becoming trapped under the front of the numnah.

Many horses hate clippers near their ears or heads. Always allow plenty of time when trimming and be prepared to work slowly and quietly to gain the horse's confidence. Charging in and putting on a nose twitch (*never* use an ear twitch) is not the answer. Try to introduce trimming as part of the daily grooming routine so it becomes normal and accepted by the horse. If clippers are not an option for trimming in this area then use a pair of sharp scissors with rounded ends. Rather than cutting horizontally across the section of mane to be removed, which results in a very jagged finish, cut lengthways up the mane. (For more information on clippers, see Clipping, later this chapter.)

The bridle path should be kept closely trimmed.

Pulling

Most Warmbloods, sports horses and horses used in English riding competitions should have their manes plaited when competing, English style, and this requires the mane to be pulled. (Plaiting is not *obligatory* in all classes so, if in doubt, check.) Pull manes to approximately 3½–4 in (9–10 cm). Never cut the mane as this leaves a blunt and generally irregular finish. Cutting combs can be used and are more humane, but it takes some practice to produce a really good finish with them. Do not wash the mane directly before pulling as the hair then becomes slippery and difficult to grasp hold of.

STEP 1
Comb through the mane, removing all tangles and laying it flat.

STEP 2
Using a mane comb (these are cheap to buy) and starting at the poll, take a small section of hair and hold the bottom firmly with your left hand. Take the mane comb and backcomb the section to the desired length until only a few strands remain in your left hand.

STEP 3
Wrap these few strands around the comb once and pull downwards sharply. Work along the length of the mane, shortening and thinning the hair in this manner.

Tip

For tidying up a pulled mane it can be helpful to use a rubber thimble on thumb and forefinger to facilitate grasping individual hairs that need to be pulled out. This also works well when pulling tails.

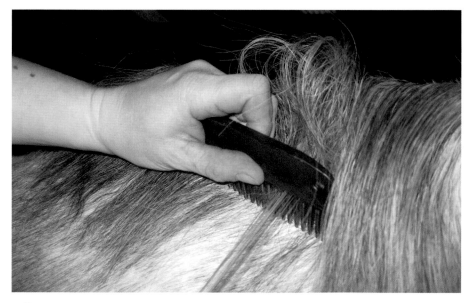

Pulling a mane, step 2.

Pull the mane after the horse has been worked, and is thus warm. The hairs will pull out more easily. Some horses are really sensitive to having their manes pulled; try giving them a haynet to take their minds off it. Spraying Chloraseptic (an anaesthetic spray used for human sore throats), or a similar product can have a numbing effect, but test it on a small piece of skin first to make sure the horse is not allergic to it.

Cutting combs are used in a similar way, but without the pulling. Back-comb the hair to the desired length and then use the cutting device on the comb. The problem with these combs is that the mane can appear very choppy unless done well, and they only shorten the mane without thinning it. If the mane is too thick then plaiting becomes difficult because either the plaits are too large, or it is necessary to put many small ones in, which is time-consuming and does not always achieve the best look.

Hogging

Hogging the mane (called roaching in the US) is when the entire mane is removed through clipping, and is kept clipped. This is frequently done on cobs, and can greatly improve the look of their neck and crest, and it is also routinely done on polo ponies to prevent the mane becoming tangled in the equipment. If the mane is hogged it will need to be re-clipped approximately every three to four weeks.

Horses that have particularly poor manes (Appaloosas tend to suffer) can

> **Tip**
>
> To keep cutting combs working well, take apart (if possible) and clean after using them. Wash with soapy water and dry the blades thoroughly, then spray with WD40 and wipe off the excess oil.

have the quality of their manes improved by hogging. Hog the mane to approximately ½–1 in (a couple of cm) from the crest in the spring. Keep the mane trimmed to this length throughout the summer, then allow it to grow out over the winter. By the following summer the mane should have grown back and generally (though not always) it will be thicker, with a better quality of hair.

STEP **1**

For the best results the horse needs to have its head stretched down to the ground – a feed bucket generally provides the encouragement needed! Starting at the withers, make one long sweep with the clippers along the middle of the crest.

STEP **2**

Repeat along either side of the crest working from withers to poll. Try to keep the number of passes with the clippers to a minimum to cut down on any chance of leaving clipper tracks.

STEP **3**

Wipe the newly clipped crest with a rag and baby oil.

Natural manes

Native pony breeds, Spanish breeds, Friesians, Saddlebreds, National Show Horses, Morgans, Arabians and some other breeds should be shown with a long natural mane. In these instances the longer and more exuberant the mane, the better. Sometimes the Spanish breeds have their manes plaited in either a Continental or running braid (see Plaiting, next section). Trying to keep very long and luxuriant manes in tip-top condition can be difficult, and the use of leave-in hair conditioner is essential. Keep combing to a minimum as it can break the hairs. Instead, use your fingers to tease through the hair, or use an old hairbrush.

Be aware when turning horses out in the summer that their coats, including the mane, are prone to sun bleaching. It can be helpful to plait long manes, then roll them up and cover in self-adhesive bandage when turning out. This prevents the hair being snagged on anything, chewed by zealous companions or being bleached by the sunlight. Alternatively, turn out with a neck cover (which can be made, see Chapter 2) but first apply leave-in conditioner so the mane does not chaff against the material.

Plaiting manes

The key to perfect English-style plaits is keeping the mane thin and pulled to a manageable length, between 3½ and 4 in (9–10 cm). Wash the mane really thoroughly four to five days before plaiting, using a good scurf-removing shampoo (for shampoo recipes, see earlier this chapter). It can be helpful at this point, and after bathing, to put the mane into bunches to get it lying on the right side if it is particularly unruly.

There are a number of products on the market designed to help keep the hair flat when plaiting. Some are better than others, and nearly all of them are expensive. Damping the mane down with good, old-fashioned water works well; make sure the hair is dampened only, not soaked. Alternatively, human hair gel can help to keep the hair flat, though it can be sticky to work with. The most economical of these are supermarket own-brands, and they can generally be picked up for not much. Use only a tiny amount.

Have the plaiting kit ready before starting and, if possible, aim to stitch plaits rather than using bands. Stitched plaits are more secure and present a more polished, finished look. Thread up plenty of needles, knot the end of each thread and push the needles through a piece of card to keep them tidy. Use blunt-ended needles, which can be bought from any needlecraft shop.

Tip

Use a clothes peg or bulldog clip to keep the mane out of the way while plaiting.

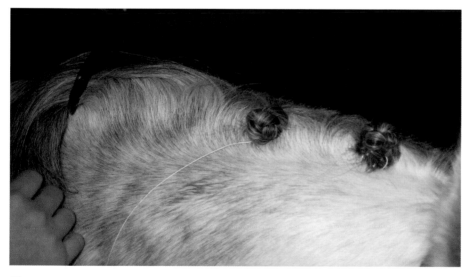

Plaiting a mane is made easier if the mane is pulled to a manageable length.

STEP **1**

Divide the mane up into bunches of between 2–2½ in (5–6.3 cm) in width and secure with elastic bands.

A word on plaits

The traditional number of plaits is 7 or 9 along the crest, plus the forelock.

Too many tiny plaits can look overdone and fussy.

Great big golf ball plaits look clumsy.

A horse with a very short neck should have smaller and more plaits to create the illusion of elegance and neck length.

A horse with a long neck should have fewer and larger plaits to shorten the overall look of the neck.

For a horse with a poor top line, sit the plaits along the top of the crest to bulk up the appearance.

For a horse with a thick neck, sit the plaits low on the crest.

STEP **2**

Starting at the poll, damp down the first bunch, divide into three sections using the mane comb and plait, pulling the plait together securely. Stitch the bottom of the plait, going from side to side, and wrapping the thread around securely.

STEP **3**

Either roll or fold the plait up to the crest and stitch in place, looping the thread from side to side for extra security.

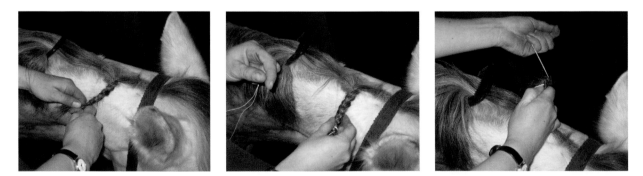

Steps in the plaiting process.

White plaits

Some riders, particularly dressage riders, favour plaits that have either white tape or special white plastic covers over them. If using these then fold the plaits rather than roll them. It is cheaper to buy white tape to use, than the white plastic covers, and the tape helps to keep the plaits secure. Some dressage judges actively dislike the white look, especially at the lower level of competitions.

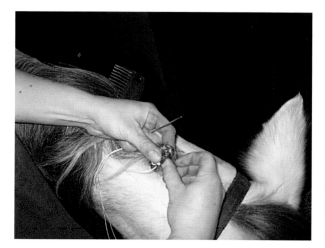 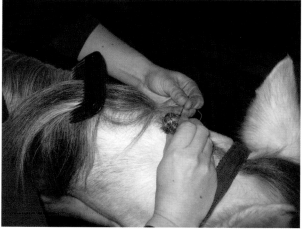

The plait is rolled or folded up, then stitched in place.

Running and Spanish plaits

These look lovely on a horse with a really long mane, but require some practice. Start a running plait at the poll and plait down the length of the crest, adding small sections of mane as the plait progresses. The poll end of the plait should follow the crest, but as it moves along the neck the plait becomes longer, and by the base it should hang down approximately 4–6 in (10–15 cm) from the crest. A Spanish plait works in the same way, but should remain tight to the crest the whole way down the mane.

Western banding

For some Western showing classes the mane is banded rather than plaited. In this case the mane still needs to be pulled, generally to between 3–5 in (7.5–12.5 cm) in length. The entire mane is divided into narrow bunches which are held in place by bands approximately 1 in (2.5 cm) down from the crest. Coloured bands are permissible in some classes.

Protecting plaits

Plaiting up is best done on the day of competition, but this is not always possible. If plaiting the night before, the plaits will need to be covered to keep them clean and tidy. This can either be done using a slinky (a type of stretchy head and neck cover made from Lycra – see Chapter 2) or using an old pair of tights. (Even if plaiting the night before, always leave the forelock and do it on the day because, no matter how careful you are, the forelock always gets dusty and messy.)

Tip

When unpicking plaits there is always a danger of cutting or damaging the mane. Invest in a proper needlework thread unpicker, these are not expensive and can be bought from any needlecraft shop. They make unpicking plaits much easier and reduce the risk of damaging the mane.

Quick plait protector

STEP **1**

Take an old pair of tights (never throw tights away) and cut one leg off.

STEP **2**

Cut the toe off the one leg and then cut the length of the leg.

STEP **3**

Lay the wide piece of nylon over the horse's crest so that the plaits and the crest are covered. Secure by placing elastic bands over each plait.

A quick and simple plait protector.

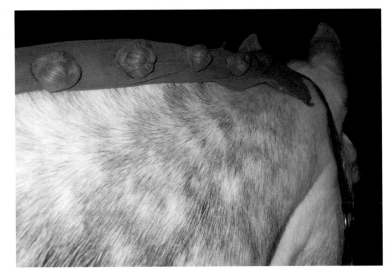

Tails

Whereas dealing with manes is pretty cut-and-dried (they are either pulled, natural or hogged) tails, and particularly their length, are more subject to fashion. Tails can either be pulled, plaited or natural. Natural tails are those that are left untouched, and for the show ring the longer they are, the better. In some Arabian classes the tails are so long that they trail the ground, but when the horse then moves the tail is held aloft and floats along behind it.

Protecting the tail hairs

The tail hairs can be quite fragile, especially in hot, dry climates, and are prone to snapping and breaking, much like long human hair. As with the

Tip

Always start brushing at the bottom of the tail or mane, not at the top, and gently remove tangles while working your way up the hair.

mane, keep brushing to an absolute minimum, and use either the fingers to tease the tail through, or an old cushioned human hairbrush. When the tail is washed, a conditioner should always be used, and leave-in conditioner should be applied on a daily basis. Be aware that some rugs can rub the top of the tail, and applying leave-in conditioner before rugging can help eliminate this. Some horses are also naturally very itchy and will rub the tail – it can even become habit-forming. First check thoroughly to ascertain the cause of the itchiness, making sure it is not a consequence of mites, lice, other infestations or allergies. Use the homemade hair conditioner with Listerine (described earlier this chapter) liberally to cut down on the itch factor, also adding chamomile or lavender to your homemade shampoo base.

Combating hair breakage

Long natural tails can be especially difficult to maintain. The ends of the tail hairs have a tendency to break off, and the ends can become very thin and wispy. The following methods can help minimise this problem.

- Keeping the tail plaited in one long plait starting from the end of the tail-bone and secured with an elastic band can help to preserve the tail hairs.

- Tail bags, which come in two types, can also be useful for preserving the tail and keeping it clean, and they are cheap and easy to make (see Chapter 2). They are best used on a tail that has been plaited as above. Insert the plait into the bag, and secure the bag using the tabs at the top, by weaving them through the top of the plait. Never tie the tags around the tailbone because it can compromise the circulation. Alternatively, some tail bags come with three sections. Divide the tail into three and thread the three sections through the individual bags, then plait the three together. Secure the bottom end of the bag with an elastic band, taking care not to pull it too tight or position it too near the bottom of the hairs, otherwise the band might cause breakage of the fragile ends.

> **Tip**
>
> Secure the end of a plait with an elastic band approximately 2 in (5 cm) from the bottom of the tail. Any lower than this and there is a danger of the band snapping off the ends of the tail hair.

Another method of protecting the long, natural tail is to keep the end bandaged.

This method of bandaging is only suitable for horses that are primarily stable-kept, since it does restrict the horse's ability to remove flies. A horse can be turned out for short periods with the tail bandaged like this, but again caution should be exercised and the turnout area/field should be free from anything that the horse's tail might get caught on. The bandage should be removed and changed once a week.

Caution

Caution should be exercised over turning a horse out wearing a tail bag. They can become hooked or caught on the fence or trees and really damage the tail if the horse pulls away. It is better to remove the bag and plait the tail into one long plait when turning out.

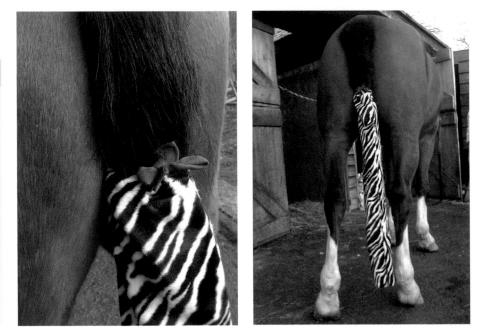

Tail bags are cheap and easy to make and useful for preserving the tail and keeping it clean.

Bandaging the end of the tail

- Starting at the end of the tailbone plait the tail in one long plait.
- Leave some wispy pieces of the tail out of the plait. This is to provide the horse with a 'fly swat'.
- Fold the plaited tail up in half.
- Starting at the end of the tail bone and using self adhesive bandage, bandage down the plaited, folded length, completely covering the plaited section.
- Be careful not to bandage in the wispy bits.

Banging, pulling and plaiting

Banging tails

Pulled and plaited tails should be presented with a neatly banged bottom, i.e., the bottom of the tail should be cut absolutely straight across. This looks very smart, but the length the tail is cut to tends to fluctuate with fashion. The traditional length for this presentation is for the tail to fall 4 in (10 cm) below the point of hock, although there has recently been a fashion for a much longer tail. In general, if the tail is too long (excepting the natural look) it tends to detract from the shape of the horse's hindquarters and can give the illusion of flattening the horse's natural cadence during movement.

To bang a tail properly first shampoo and condition it, and then gently brush through, removing all tangles. Have an assistant place their arm under the tailbone and raise the tail to the level of natural carriage for the horse (some horses carry their tails much higher during movement than others). Run one hand down the length of the tail and with the other trim the hair straight across approximately 4 in (10 cm) below the point of hock. Use either very sharp scissors, or clippers. If using scissors, try to make the cut in one go to prevent an irregular look. The bottom of the tail should be absolutely straight across, and generally when cut like this, the tail will be given an illusion of thickness.

Pulling tails

A well-pulled tail can be very smart, but requires regular maintenance to keep it looking good. As with pulling manes, aim to pull the tail after the horse has been worked, and is warm – the hairs will pull out more easily and the horse should be more relaxed. The tail should be pulled to accentuate the shape of the hindquarters (producing the same effect that a plaited tail does) and, as a guide, when standing behind the horse it should be pulled down to the point where the hindquarters start to curve away from you. Aim to pull the tail over a few weeks; it is a painful process and should be done in short instalments. Pull a few hairs from underneath and either side of the top of the tailbone, leaving those at the top slightly longer than those in the middle section. Using rubber thimbles on the thumb and forefinger can help in grasping the hairs. Once the tail has been pulled try to bandage it for a couple of hours every day to help maintain the shape, and regularly pull and remove hairs as they start to grow out.

Plaiting tails

There are two methods of plaiting tails; one produces a flat plait and the other a raised plait. The latter is the harder to do and requires some prac-tice! As with plaiting manes, some people find gel products help to keep the hairs lying flat, although personally I find that water works just as well. Shampoo the tail at least four days prior to plaiting so that the hair is not too slippery.

STEP **1**

Brush through the tail and remove all tangles. Dampen the top of the tail and take three small portions of hair, two from one side and one from the other.

STEP **2**

Begin to plait down taking a small section of hair from each side of the tailbone as you work your way down. If you pass each section over the top of the other while plaiting it produces a flat plait; if the sections are passed underneath however, it produces a raised plait.

STEP **3**

Plait down the tailbone in this way until you reach the point at which the quarters slope away from you. Then continue the plait down without taking more sections of hair. Stitch the end of the plait and then fold the end up to make a loop and stitch together. Some people prefer a rosebud finish, in which case instead of folding the plait, roll it up and stitch securely.

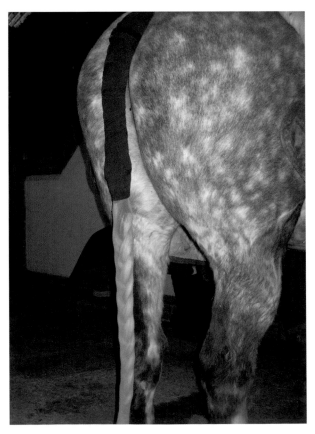

Using an old pair of tights to protect the tail plait.

Hairspray can be used to keep any small hairs in check, but exercise caution when using aerosols around horses.

Protecting the plait

One of the best ways to protect the plait and the end of the tail is by using an old pair of tights. Cut one leg off the tights and then cut the toe off. Roll the tight leg up and thread over the tail, then roll down to cover the tail. Secure in place with a tail bandage over the top half, and fasten the bottom end with an elastic band.

Bathing and grooming

Regular bathing through the summer and when the weather and/or facilities permit will keep the coat clean and in good condition, provided the horse is receiving a healthy and balanced diet. Use a common-sense approach to bathing the grass-kept horse. Regular bathing will strip the coat of its natural oil, which the horse kept out will need, so bath only when really necessary, or when the weather is warm enough that the horse will dry quickly without chilling. For the stabled horse, regular bathing is fine. Horses should be washed down following exercise to remove dried sweat from the coat anyway, and instead of using plain water, it can be useful instead to give them a quick bath, adding a little shampoo and rinsing well.

Bathing using warm water is preferable; it is more pleasant for the horse, particularly after exercise if the muscles are at all tight, and is conducive to a cleaner finish. If warm water facilities are not available on the stable yard, it is possible to buy hose adapters that will fit over a normal house tap. The hose can then be run out of a kitchen window or similar. These fittings are generally available fairly cheaply from a good hardware shop. Also attach a fitting to the other end of the hose that allows the flow of water to be temporarily turned off (without going back to the tap). This will minimise the amount of water wasted, and is particularly relevant in respect of energy consumption if hot water is being used. Also when bathing, be aware of the area you are using. Most people do not have access to purpose-built wash stalls and have to make do. If this is the case then try to use an area of hard standing, or gravel, and avoid dirt/mud, and if possible position the horse near either an equine-friendly drain, or on an area where the water can drain away without creating too much of a mud hole.

Bathing kit

It is helpful to assemble a bathing kit and then keep it together so it is easily accessible. Either keep it in an old feed/supplement bucket or a container (trying if possible to use a recycled plastic one). Be sure to have a cooler to hand to place over the horse as it dries off, to prevent chilling down unless the weather is very warm. The kit should include:

- Three sponges, preferably different colours. Keep one for the eyes and nose, one for under the dock, and a large one for soaping the body. Sponges can be bought very cheaply from car accessory shops, hardware shops or even supermarkets.

- Sweat scraper. Either metal or rubber, to remove excess water from the coat after bathing. Generally, sweat scrapers can be bought very cheaply. Otherwise make a cup with your hand, holding the fingers rigid, and using strong, downward strokes pass your hand over the coat. This is not as effective as using a sweat scraper but does work if you are in a bind. Similarly cut a length of baling twine approximately 2 ft (61 cm) in length, wrap an end round each hand and pass over the coat, applying firm pressure. Alternatively, an old plastic-shafted short whip can work quite well as a sweat scraper.

- Adapters for both ends of the hose, one to fit to the tap and one to turn the flow of water off at the end of the hose. Garden spray nozzles are very good, especially those with adjustable spray patterns.

- Shampoo, preferably homemade as described earlier this chapter. If the coat is thoroughly washed and rinsed, it should not be necessary to use a conditioner on the body hair as well, instead use a spray-on leave-in conditioner. If homemade shampoo is not an option there are a number of very reasonable shampoos marketed by various supermarkets under their own brand name. Remember to never throw out old plastic bottles; they can always be re-used!

- Leave-in conditioners, preferably homemade. One branded product does deserve mention and that is Show Sheen, in my experience it outclasses all other products of a similar nature. This leave-in conditioner is expensive, but is extremely effective, particularly for use on tails that are prone to tangling. If using a leave-in hair conditioner, do not spray on the saddle area!

- Rinses. These are used in the rinse water and do not need to be further rinsed out. Rinses can be made to enhance shiny coats, for dry coats, oily coats and to soothe tired muscles (see How to Make Rinses, below).

- Towels. Old house towels can be recycled to the stable yard and used for removing the worst of the water.

- Water brush for scrubbing the feet, and a hoof pick. Always pick the feet out before bathing the horse and give them a good scrub to remove any dried-on dirt or mud. Avoid the heel areas if possible, or for horses with particularly sensitive skin, apply a thin layer of Vaseline to the heels first before washing the feet and legs.

- A rubber mitt or a rubber curry comb can be a useful addition to a bathing kit, particularly for removing thick dirt, mud or dead hair.

How to make rinses

There is actually very little involved once the ingredients have been assembled. First rinse the soap from the coat thoroughly, using the hose. The pressure from the hose will greatly aid proper rinsing. Once all traces of soap have been removed from the coat, fill one or two buckets with warm water.

The rinse aid will then be added to this, and does not need to be further rinsed out.

For shiny coats

Add two cupfuls of white vinegar to the water. Vinegar in the rinse water leaves the coat really smooth and shiny; it is one of the cheapest and oldest tricks to produce a perfect shiny coat.

For dry coats

Add one or two capfuls of baby oil to the rinse water, or one capful of olive oil. Both help with scurfy or dry coats, but don't be tempted to add too much otherwise the coat will appear greasy. If the dry condition is causing the horse to itch (and provided veterinary advice is not needed), then try adding a capful of mouthwash along with the baby oil to the rinse water.

For scurfy coats

A rosemary infusion is good for helping clear up scurf. Add one tbsp (15 ml) of dried rosemary to 1½ pints (0.85 litre) of water and bring to the boil. Cover and simmer for 3 minutes, then strain off the rosemary and use the liquid, once cooled, as a post-shampooing rinse.

For oily coats

Vinegar is good for oily coats. Also, combine two cupfuls of white vinegar with the juice from one lemon, but be aware that lemon juice can have a lightening effect on dark-coloured coats.

For dark coats

Adding a capful of baby oil to the rinse water will really bring the colour and shine out on dark bays, blacks and liver chestnuts.

For sun-bleached coats

All coats are susceptible to sun-bleaching, although it is most obvious on dark coats and the hairs will bleach and fade if exposed for any length of time. To try to bring shine and lustre back to a sun-bleached coat, use a cupful of white vinegar and a cupful of olive oil in the rinse water.

For greys

Add a capful of bluing solution to the rinse water. Make sure that you do not use more than one capful per three gallons (13.5 litres), and patch test the skin first as some horses may be sensitive to it.

Bathing and grooming tips

How to keep white tails white

Greys tend to be the most muck-loving horses around and are notoriously difficult to keep clean. White tails, especially, can be really difficult to keep sparkling white. Try using homemade shampoo with lemon oil (see Shampoo for Greasy Coats, earlier this chapter), or use the juice from one lemon and the grated rind combined with the shampoo base. A less eco-friendly alternative is to wash the ends of the tail with a non-biological washing powder. These are really effective in removing stains, but can be an irritant, so be careful not to get them on the dock or skin, but only on the long tail hairs. Another method is to use washing-up liquid in the water, and then soak the tail for as long as possible (by holding up a bucket). Again, try not to get the soap on the dock or skin, and when rinsing make sure that all trace of the detergent is rinsed out. Human hair products for silver/grey hair, such as silvering shampoo, also work well: they can be expensive, but you only need to use a small amount so they do last quite well. One of the best ways to keep tails white is to try to keep them as clean as possible all the time, rather than allowing them to become too yellowed. Do this by keeping the tail in a tail bag (for instructions on making one, see Chapter 2) where possible and when stabled.

Other tips for shiny coats

The quality of the horse's coat is a reflection of the overall health of the horse, and provided it is receiving a balanced and healthy diet its coat should naturally be in good condition. However, for the show-quality shine try:

- Keeping all brushes regularly washed to prevent build-up of grease and scurf.

- Giving the horse a warm bath can help to dislodge the dead winter coat. Use a rubber mitt, a rubber curry comb or even an old rubber glove to work the dead coat out.

- Keeping rugs and blankets washed and clean will help.

- The use of a 'slinky' can be very helpful in keeping the coat shiny. They act as a barrier against dirt and dust in the stable, and also polish the coat hairs as a product of their tight fit.

- Feed a supplement of linseed oil. Linseed is an old-fashioned but excellent additive to produce a shiny coat. Make sure it is prepared properly. If bought in its raw state, linseed MUST be soaked overnight in cold water, then add more water so that the linseed is covered by approximately 1 in (2.5 cm) and boil vigorously for several minutes. Allow it to simmer until it turns into a jelly-like consistency then let it cool before feeding it. Only prepare as much as you will use because it quickly turns rancid. (It is now possible to buy linseed ready prepared; this should be fed according to the manufacturer's directions.)

- Feed corn oil or vegetable oil. This will improve the shine on the coat, but be aware that oils are also a source of fat, and so are not suitable for horses prone to laminitis or those that carry too much weight. When feeding oil as a supplement for the coat, do not use more than 3½ fl oz (100 ml) a day.

- Including strapping as part of the daily grooming routine helps to maintain the horse's (and your own!) muscles and keep the coat looking really good. See below for making your own strapping pad. After first thoroughly grooming the horse to remove dirt, start at the top of the neck and, working your way down and across the major muscle masses of the horse (avoiding any bony areas), bring the pad down firmly with one hand, and using a polishing cloth smooth the area over with the other hand. Build up a rhythm of banging and smoothing.

- For a last-minute shine before entering a show ring, pass either a tumble dryer conditioning sheet or a baby wipe over the horse. These are cheap to buy and will pick up any specks of dust.

- Aerosol furniture polish can be used on the coat and tail, although be sure to patch-test an area on the horse first and leave overnight to make sure there is no allergic reaction. Spray the polish onto a clean cloth and pass over the neck and quarters of the horse for shine, and spray the bottom end of the tail. Be aware that not all horses appreciate aerosols! Also make sure that the horse is thoroughly bathed after the show to remove the polish.

How to make a strapping pad

While leather strapping pads can be quite expensive to buy, they are easy to make, but only if you have suitable needles and thread for working with leather.

YOU WILL NEED

Two pieces of reasonably thin leather, or suede (try asking local saddlers, or even
  upholstery companies for off-cuts)

One piece of either strong webbing or slightly thicker leather

Stuffing material, old tights, socks or shredded T-shirts work well, or proper
  stuffing material available from needlecraft shops

Strong thread suitable for use with leather

A leather needle

A thimble

STEP 1

Cut two oval shapes from the leather or suede. These need to be approximately 8 x 4 in (20 x 10 cm).

STEP 2

Take a piece of strong webbing approximately 6 in (15 cm) long by 1 in (2.5 cm) wide, or cut a slightly thicker piece of leather to the same dimensions. This will form the 'handle'. Stitch this piece in the centre, horizontally, of one of the oval pieces, allowing enough room to fit your hand under the strap.

STEP 3

Stitch the two oval pieces together, making sure that the handle is to the outside (!) and leaving a small gap at one end.

STEP 4

Insert the stuffing, taking care to make sure it is packed very tightly and leaves a smooth finish. There must be no irregularities or unevenness. Sew up the hole and you are ready to get strapping.

How to make a grooming mitt

The polishing part of the strapping process is very important; it relaxes the muscle mass and improves the shine of the coat. Old tea towels or soft cotton T-shirts can be used as polishing clothes, or alternatively use a grooming mitt. There are generally not terribly expensive to buy but, again, are easy to make.

YOU WILL NEED

Two pieces of synthetic sheepskin

A piece of paper and a marker pen

Needle and strong thread

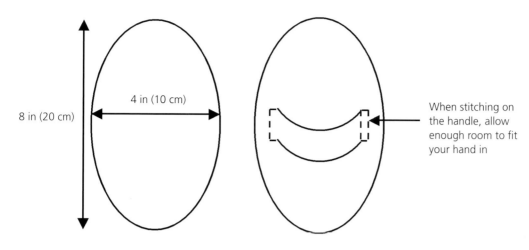

8 in (20 cm)

4 in (10 cm)

When stitching on the handle, allow enough room to fit your hand in

Making a strapping pad.

STEP **1**

Lay your hand on the piece of paper and draw an 'oven glove' type outline around your hand. Then cut around the outline to produce a template.

STEP **2**

Place the template on the synthetic sheepskin (it is preferable to use synthetic sheepskin rather than the real thing because it is easier to wash, and grooming mitts must be kept clean and washed otherwise it defeats the purpose of the exercise!). Cut out two pieces of the sheepskin (one pile-out, one pile-in) and place them on top of each other with the pile to the inside on both mitts.

STEP **3**

Stitch around the perimeter, leaving the bottom open. Turn the right way out and there is your grooming mitt. *See photos overleaf* ▶

Clipping

There are few things that look quite so bad as a poorly clipped horse! Generally the stabled horse, or horse in work, is clipped during the winter months to allow the horse to be worked hard and still dry off quickly, and to minimise loss of condition. A clipped horse is also easier to keep clean. Dependent on the horse, the climate and the work the horse is in, the first clip of the season would normally be needed around September time. If the

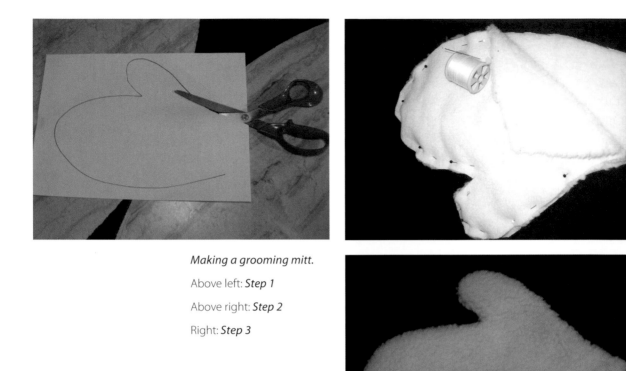

Making a grooming mitt.

Above left: *Step 1*

Above right: *Step 2*

Right: *Step 3*

horse is only to be clipped during the winter, try not to clip again after January/February time, which is when the summer coat will be starting to come through. Some horses are kept clipped year round: clipping in the summer is beneficial for horses in very hard, fast work, horses that overheat, some older horses and some horses for show classes (in particular Arabian classes).

Preparing for the perfect clip

The clippers

Before turning to the horse, make sure that your clippers are in good working order and that the blades are sharp. Clippers are expensive, but if at all possible it is worth spending money on them. The better quality the clipper and the blades, the longer they last and the better finish they will give.

It is worth looking into buying second-hand clippers. Provided that they are a good-quality make they should be fine, although they might need to be sent for a service. Send blades off for re-sharpening at the end of the season and always clip using two blades, so they can be switched over when they start to heat up.

One source of equestrian products that can be good is eBay, although caution should be exercised. If purchasing from eBay do a thorough background check on the seller, and even if they have a high rating, check to see what products they have been selling to gain their rating. An eBay seller's trick is to sell hundreds of small, cheap items for a few pounds, in order to gain a high rating, and then sell an expensive item and con the purchaser. They can then close their account and set up a new one and start the procedure again.

Preparing and finishing off the coat

Preparing the coat before clipping can make a vast difference to the overall finished result.

Thoroughly bath the horse in warm water and remove all traces of grease, dirt and scurf. The more thorough the bath, the better. The real trick however, is to use a bucket or two of warm rinse water with one cupful of olive oil added. The oil makes the coat slippery and smooth, and greatly improves the clip.

After bathing, dry the horse and then put a full body, head and neck slinky on to keep the coat as clean as possible, then clip the following day.

Following clipping, soak a rag in a solution of washing soda (one handful to a bucket of warm water) and pass over the horse from head to toe – this helps to remove any 'tram lines'.

Tips for clipping

- Use good-quality clippers and blades, and blades that are sharp.
- Only clip in an area that has a good light source, and preferably on rubber mats, or at least hard standing.
- Always use a circuit breaker.
- Keep blades oiled.
- Switch blades when they get too hot.
- Clip using long sweeps with the clippers, rather than short passes.

- Bandage the tail out of the way before clipping and put mane hair into bunches.

- If doing a blanket clip, take a piece of baling twine and tie a knot in the middle, trim either side of the knot so the string is equal lengths on both sides, and the desired length that you wish the blanket part of the clip to be. Place knot on the spine and allow the two ends to drape on either side of the horse and make a mark. This way the blanket clip will be even on each side.

- Draw the outline of the clip you want using a water-based marker pen, saddle soap or chalk.

Tips for turnout

Many of the things that we do to keep our horses healthy, tidy and presentable can be extended or elaborated upon to present a truly eye-catching picture in the show ring.

- Clip the ears to remove any tufts of hair. Squeeze the two sides of the ear together and run the clippers down the edge from the ear tip down. (Horses that are kept out should not have the insides of their ears completely clipped as the hair provides some protection against flies and midges.)

- For horses with black points or dark ears, leave a small tuft on the tip of the ear to the inside edge, this accentuates the shape and elegance of the ear.

- For horses with very short ears, clip the hair on the ears but leave a tuft at the tip, this creates a false tip and gives the impression of the ear being longer than it is.

- Before entering the show ring run a rag with baby oil on it around the inside of the ears to darken them.

- Hide any white marks, blemishes, or scars in the ears with appropriate coloured shoe polish.

- Clip the bridle path the day before a show, making a 1 in (2.5 cm) margin for horses in English classes, 4–5 in (10–12.5 cm) for Quarter Horses being ridden in Western disciplines, and 6–8 in (15–20 cm) for Arabs.

- Clip the straggly hairs that grow across the withers.

Tip

Remember to remove all oil and other 'cosmetic' applications from the horse directly after the competition.

- Turn the clippers upside down and run in the direction of hair growth down the back of the cannon bones and around the knees and fetlocks if the horse is prone to 'hairy' legs.

- Clipping completely the white hair on a horse with socks or stockings improves the look of the legs and makes them appear whiter.

- Clipping white markings on the face also increases their distinction, but be careful not to run the clippers over onto the coloured hairs.

- Turn the clippers upside down and trim the hair around the coronary band so it is in a nice straight line.

- Run the clippers in the direction of hair growth along the jaw and chin to improve the definition of the jaw line.

- Clip away the long 'eyebrow' hairs.

- Clip or shave all muzzle hairs (see below) on the morning of the show.

- Apply baby oil, Vaseline or face paint around the eyes, on the inside of the ears, around the muzzle including into the nostrils, and (using a different rag), under the tailbone.

- Directly before entering the ring, apply quarter markings (see below), shark's teeth and buttock marks, provided that your horse has adequate conformation. If the horse is slightly weak behind do not draw attention to this area by applying markings! Spray with hairspray to fix the hair in place.

- Wash and scrub the feet inside and out before the show (see below for perfect feet).

- Immediately prior to entering the ring, pass a tumble dryer conditioning cloth or baby wipe over the horse to remove any specks of dust.

Keeping white bits white

- Greys, and horses with white markings, are notoriously prone to covering themselves in as much muck and grime as possible. Bathing greys with a bluing solution can help to remove stains and produce a brilliant white effect.

- Biological washing powder is excellent for getting rid of stains, but is quite caustic, so only use it on the ends of the tail and do not bring into contact with the horse's skin.

- Alternatively, use a tiny amount of non-biological washing powder (which is not as caustic but still fairly effective at stain reduction) when bathing, though be sure to do a small allergy test first.

- Corn starch or baby powder can be used to brighten the leg hairs at the last minute.

- Chalk is useful for covering up last-minute stains, as is a small amount of white shoe polish.

- There are products available specifically for enhancing white markings and for concealing stains. Generally they work fairly well, although they are expensive. The old-fashioned methods listed above do the job just as well!

- See also How to Keep White Tails White earlier this chapter.

How to hide scars and blemishes

- Shoe polish of the appropriate colour is useful for hiding small scars and blemishes, but if the blemish is too big then it is better to leave it alone. Judges do not appreciate running a hand over a horse and getting covered in shoe polish or other blemish-concealing products!

- Applying Vaseline to scars will encourage the hair to grow back, as will vitamin E cream.

- Shoe polish to darken the insides of the ears is useful (always wipe the product off after use).

- Chalk and/or baby powder can be useful for hiding small scars and stains on greys.

Whiskers

For showing, whiskers need to be removed, and preferably at the last minute as they grow back at an alarming rate.

Trim long, unsightly hairs from around the jawbone using clippers in the direction of hair growth.

Whiskers around the muzzle can be removed using clippers or trimmers, working against the direction of hair growth.

Wet shaving using disposable razors is another very effective method, and can be done literally on the day of the show. Dampen a rag and moisten the muzzle area (or use a little baby oil) before shaving the hairs off against the direction of growth, taking care not to nick the horse.

Caution

Always exercise caution when applying Vaseline or oil to the horse for showing as, under bright sunlight, these products will increase the chance of sunburn for the horse – particularly relevant for horses with pink skin pigment. Always remove oils and grease immediately after the show, or use a cream with sunblock in it.

Quarter marks

Quarter markings come in a variety of different patterns including chevrons, diamonds, stars and squares, although some people use highly imaginative and elaborate ones. Normally, quarter-marking sheets are quite reasonable to buy, and can be fiddly to make, however making your own allows scope for custom patterns.

How to make quater-marking sheets

YOU WILL NEED

A sheet of pliable plastic (preferably recycled!) – try local hardware shops or DIY
  stores (use a sheet of appropriate size to the size of the horse/pony)
A ruler and a marker pen
A template
A sharp Stanley knife or pair of pointed needlecraft scissors
A piece of board and four small nails or tacks

> **Tip**
>
> Quarter markings can also be made freehand using a fine-toothed comb. Lice combs are particularly good!

It makes life much easier if it is possible to secure the piece of plastic to prevent it moving while working on it. If you have access to a large piece of board (and it doesn't matter if it gets scored) lay the plastic flat on the board and secure with a small nail or tack in each corner. Next decide on the pattern you wish to make – for example a star pattern. Draw or trace the star onto a piece of paper and cut it out to form a template. Then mark the sheet of plastic with horizontal and vertical lines to fit the dimensions of the star. This is to ensure that the pattern is even. Trace the outline onto the plastic, repeatedly in rows (you can decide on the size and number of patterns to appear on the sheet in relation to the size and stamp of the horse). Next comes the difficult bit! Cut out the pattern using the Stanley knife or scissors, making sure all edges are smooth and regular. This is not a project for impatient people! *See photos overleaf* ▶

Perfect quarter marks

Make sure the coat is clean and free from dust, dirt and scurf. Using a stiff brush, brush the hair from the hip towards the tail. Place the sheet with its top edge running along the spine and, holding it firmly in place with one hand, with the other hand brush the hair downwards through the sheet. Lift the sheet off carefully so as not to disturb the pattern and spray the hair with hairspray to hold.

Equipment for making quarter markers.

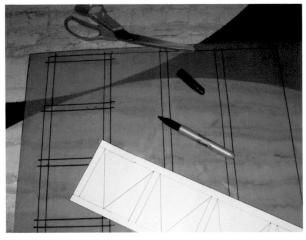

Drawing the pattern.

The pattern marked out on the plastic sheet.

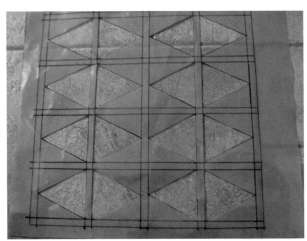

The patterns cut out.

It is possible to make markings without using a sheet. Brush the hair towards the tail then take a small comb (a cheap human one is fine) and pull the hair downwards in the desired pattern using the comb. This method allows slightly more flexibility, but it is also quite difficult to achieve a regular pattern.

Show feet

Hoof oil should only ever be used when showing as it dries the feet and is detrimental to the quality of the horn. When preparing the feet for showing, first pick them out, then scrub them thoroughly including the underneath, but taking care with the heel bulb area. Next take a fine (or finishing) sanding block, which can be bought from DIY shops for next to nothing, and run lightly over the exterior of the hoof. Once the entire wall feels smooth to the touch the hooves are ready for oiling. It is helpful to have an old square of carpet, or recycle a rubber car mat, to place the horse's hoof on when oiling. Fast-drying oils are the best, although shoe polish can also be used. Following the show apply a hoof salve to the feet to negate the effect of the sanding and the drying effect of the oil.

Tip

You can use boot polish rather than hoof oil. Often it is cheaper and lasts longer.

CHAPTER 2

Horse clothing

Rugs, sheets and coolers

There is a huge range of rugs on the market produced from increasingly technical and sophisticated materials, and available in every conceivable colour combination. For the most part these rugs do not come cheaply. Manufacturers are, however, now paying much better attention to fit, and the materials themselves with their heating, cooling and moisture-wicking properties are at the leading edge of their field. So what does this all mean to the thrifty horse lover, and is it possible to make to your own for a fraction of the cost? The answer is yes and no. It *is* possible to make a number of different types of rugs, and generally for less money than they would cost to buy. Alternatively old rugs can be revamped, 'blinged up' and recycled. Making your own is rewarding and can be cheaper. There are exceptions though, and sometimes the cost of purchasing the material and the time factor involved in making the rug does not balance out against the expenditure of simply buying it. This applies particularly to waterproof turnout rugs, and spending some money on a good waterproof rug is, in the long term, sensible. The fabrics now used are incredibly advanced, and not readily available to buy in swatches. The commercially produced rugs are also generally very well designed, conforming to the horse and remaining in place during energetic activity. For the average needle person (one end is sharp, the other blunt) creating patterns to equate with these is just too complicated. The same has to be said for hoods, where the fit must be absolutely correct to prevent slipping. So although it is possible to make these, again spending the money on buying a properly crafted one is worth it.

If you decide to buy rugs rather than making them, the financial saving comes from shopping around. eBay can be a good source of equestrian products provided caution is used. Always go for a known brand of rug, preferably with tags on, and be sure to check the cost of postage and packaging. Warehouse shops are another good source for equestrian products, and are generally advertised in equestrian magazines or local newspapers. Sometimes stands at horse shows have offers on, although they occasionally raise their prices in order to drop them and stick a sale ticket on. Price-check on the internet and compare prices to those of your local shops. Also think ahead – often tack shops will put winter rugs on sale in the spring and vice versa. Companies like Argos and some of the big supermarkets now stock equestrian equipment – but always check the quality of the product.

Measuring for rugs and making a pattern

Rugs are measured in 3 in (7.5 cm) increments. To measure a horse for a rug, run a tape measure from the centre of the chest horizontally round to the point of buttock.

If making a rug for a horse, there are several different measurements that need to be made; these sound complicated, but when looked at in conjunction with the diagram they become clear.

However, the easiest way to make a pattern for a rug is to find a rug that fits the horse well and then make a pattern directly from this. This cuts out all the fiddly measuring!

Rough guide sizing chart

Horse/pony size	Rug size (ft/in)	Rug size (cm)
11.2–12.0 hh	4′9″	145
12.0–13.0 hh	5′0″	152
13.0–14.0 hh	5′3″	160
14.0–14.2 hh	5′6″	168
14.2–15.0 hh	5′9″	175
15.0–15.2 hh	6′0″	183
15.2–16.0 hh	6′3″	190
16.0–16.2 hh	6′6″	200
16.2 hh and over	6′9″	206

Tip

Small areas of the traditional style New Zealand rug can be re-proofed using waterproof coat wax.

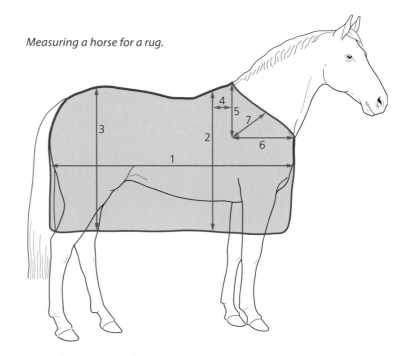

Measuring a horse for a rug.

1. From the centre of the chest to the point of buttock.

2. The depth vertically from the highest point of the withers to the lower edge of where the rug will end, generally several inches below the belly.

3. The depth vertically from the croup to the lower edge of where the rug will end.

4. Horizontally from the highest point of the withers to where the front of the neck of the rug will lie.

5. From the front of the neck of the rug vertically down until level with the bottom of the front of the neck.

6. Horizontally from the bottom of the front of the neck of the rug across to the line in 5.

7. Diagonally from where 5 and 6 intersect to the curve of the neck of the rug.

How much material?

The amount of material depends entirely on the size of the horse, and the beauty of making your own made-to-measure rug is that you can add or shorten the depth or length dependent on the horse's shape.

A standard *depth* of rug – i.e. measurement (3) for a 16 hh horse (summer sheet, sweat rug, day rug) is approximately 36 in (90 cm). Night rugs and coolers might be slightly deeper.

A standard *length* of rug – i.e. measurement (1) for a 16 hh horse is approximately 6 ft (183 cm).

So you will need twice the depth + the length.

To work out how much binding is needed for rugs that are to be completely bound take 3x the length + 4x depth + 36 in (90 cm): this gives a generous allowance, but extra binding can always be used for making filet string attachments.

Converting duvets, sleeping bags and blankets into rugs

The steps for turning duvets, blankets and sleeping bags into rugs, are basically the same, with a few alterations dependent on the type of rug required.

Turning a duvet into a rug

This is a really easy way to make an effective and warm under-blanket for next to nothing. Either use an old double duvet, or purchase a really cheap double duvet from one of the large supermarkets, often for just a few pounds.

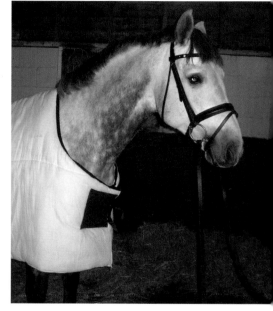

With care, and a few alterations, all sorts of human bedding can be converted into rugs.

YOU WILL NEED

A standard size old double duvet (which will convert into a 6 ft (183 cm) rug
68 in (173 cm) of 1½ in (3.8 cm) wide binding for trimming front, plus two
   8 in (20 cm) pieces for making filet string loops
Two pieces of old jeans material or similar weight fabric
Strap and buckle
Filet string

STEP **1**
Fold the duvet in half, lengthways and lay it on the floor (or large table). Take a rug that fits the horse and lay it on top of the duvet.

STEP **2**
Using a marker pen, trace the curved outline for the neck of the rug onto the duvet. Turn the duvet over and do the same on the other side, so the outline now forms a half-circle.

STEP **3**
Cut away following the shape of the marked line but leaving a 1 in (2.5 cm) margin. Then carefully remove the internal padding that falls directly to the marked line – this will make stitching on the trim much easier.

Tip

One fastening is sufficient, but two are better and will help to keep the rug in position more efficiently. Save fastenings from old rugs and recycle onto new ones.

STEP 4

Pin the two sides together and stitch along the marked line. Once the two sides are sewn together trim off the excess hem – what remains will be covered by the trim.

STEP 5

Either the whole of the outside rim of the duvet can be edged with trim, or just the neckpiece to cover the stitching. If trimming the entire rug, start at the centre of the back edge of the rug. Position the trim on the outside of the rug along the edge with approximately one-third of the trim projecting above the rug edge. Sew in place.

STEP 6

Turn the rug over and fold the trim down to cover the edge. (It can be helpful to iron it down). Now stitch this down.

STEP 7

Stitch a patch of heavy cotton or old jeans material on each side of the front of the rug, and then stitch your fastenings to this. Strap and buckle fastenings work well, although it is possible to use Velcro as long as it is really heavy-duty and sticky. You can reinforce this by using extra pieces of material on the inside.

STEP 8

Take two 8 in (20 cm) pieces of trim, fold each one in half and then fold the loose ends back on themselves by another inch (2.5 cm). Stitch each one on the inside of the rug at the back, sewing round the 1 in (2.5 cm) section. These are the loops to which the filet can be attached.

Below and opposite page: Turning a duvet into a rug.

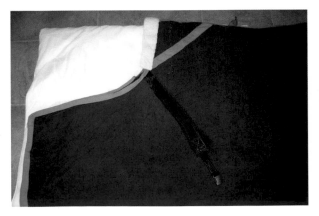

Step 1

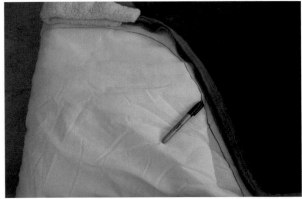

Step 2

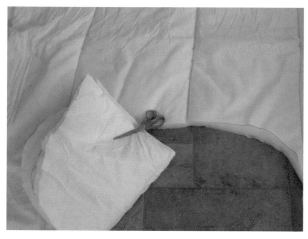

Step 3

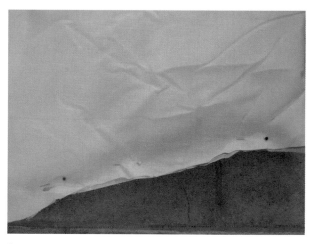

Step 4

Step 4 continued

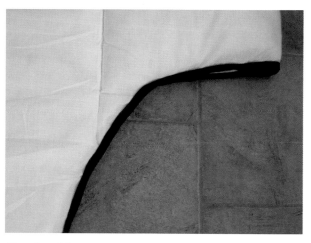

Steps 5 and 6

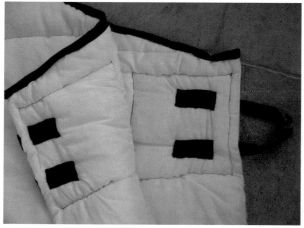

Step 7

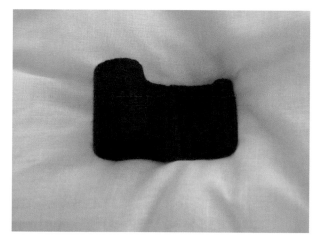

Step 8

Tip

Always use pins with brightly coloured heads and count how many you have used on the material to make sure that none are accidentally left in to poke the horse.

Stitching on binding can be quite fiddly, but it does give the rug a nice finished look. Take care when making corners with the binding, and fold the material in on itself, then stitch diagonally along the new seam.

Since the duvet rug is used as an under-blanket it is generally not necessary to put on cross-straps, but this is always an option particularly if your horse is very mobile in the stable and the rugs have a tendency to slip.

Turning sleeping bags into under-rugs

The old-fashioned rectangular sleeping rugs can also be easily converted into quilted under-rugs, using similar steps to those outlined above in respect of duvets. Old sleeping bags can often be found in charity shops for next to no money, or lurking in the attic!

YOU WILL NEED
An old sleeping bag
68 in (173 cm) of 1½ in (3.8 cm) wide binding for trimming the front plus two
8 in (20 cm) pieces for making filet string loops
Two pieces of jeans material or heavy duty cotton
Strap and buckle
Filet string

Tip

Never throw any pieces of old equipment away. Rugs can always be recycled or have their buckles and straps removed and used on new items. Similarly, old tack can be broken down and used for repairing newer items.

STEP **1**
Unzip the sleeping bag and, taking a sharp pair of scissors, cut away the zip all the way around. Next re-fold the sleeping bag in half and lay it flat on the floor, then take a rug that fits the horse and lay it on top of the sleeping bag.

STEP **2**
Is the same as for the duvet: using a marker pen, trace the cube outline for the neck of the rug onto the sleeping bag, turning the bag over and marking the other side as well, so the outline now forms a half-circle.

STEP **3**
Cut away following the shape of the marked line but leaving a 1 in (2.5 cm) margin. Then carefully remove the internal padding (if necessary) that lies directly to the marked line – this will make stitching on the trim much easier.

STEP **4**
Pin the two sides together starting at the top of the neck and working all the way back to join the sides where the zip has been removed. Then stitch together and trim away any excess hem.

STEP **5**

It is not *necessary* to add trim to these under-blankets, particularly if you are in a hurry, but it does make the rug look much better. If you decide to add trim then start at the centre of the back and the lay the trim on the outside of the edge of the rug with approximately one-third of the trim projecting above the rug edge. Sew in place.

Follow steps six through eight from the duvet section.

Trimming corners

Fold the trim around the corner to produce a mitre effect then sew diagonally along the fold.

Converting bed blankets to rugs

An old-fashioned woollen bed blanket can be easily converted to make a really useful rug that can either be used as an under-blanket to provide an extra layer, or as a day rug, travelling rug or cooler. Again the basic steps are all very similar.

YOU WILL NEED

A double bed blanket of reasonable weight
34 ft (10.4 m) of 1½ in (3.8 cm) wide binding for a 6 ft 6 in (2 m) rug
Two pieces of jeans material, or similar
Strap and buckle fastening
Cross-straps if required
Filet string

STEP **1**

Lay the double blanket out flat on the floor and cut in half lengthways so you have two pieces of material. Next, measure out the rug pattern, or trace the outline of an existing rug on both pieces of material. When cutting the material, leave an approximately 1 in (2.5 cm) margin above your marked line along the top edge; this is to allow material to make the seam that joins the two pieces together.

STEP **2**

Pin the two halves of the rug together and carefully try on the horse to make sure the top seam is lying correctly. Make any adjustments necessary. Stitch the two pieces together to create a flat seam. Take two pieces of binding 16 in (40.5 cm) long and position them onto the central seam 12 in (30 cm) back from the front of the rug. Position them diagonally so they join the front of rug along the neckline.

STEP 3

Next, position the back cross-straps with their uppermost ends on the central seam. The short strap, approximately 30 in (76 cm), should be on the left side of the rug; the long strap, approximately 72 in (183 cm) should be on the right side.

STEP 4

Take a 57 in (145 cm) piece of trim and pin over the central seam, the ends of the two 16 in (40.5 cm) pieces, and the ends of the two back cross-straps. Stitch down securely using three rows of stitches.

STEP 5

Take the two pieces of heavier cotton material and stitch on the inside shoulder area of the rug – these will bolster up the rug in the area where the fastenings are attached. Alternatively, use the material left over from cutting out the neck section of the rug and stitch this in place instead.

If necessary, you can stitch darts into the rug to improve the fit. These can be useful in the shoulder area to make the rug sit correctly, or on the back edge to make the material curve over the buttocks. Darts should always be stitched on the outside of the rug so they do not create pressure points. Make the dart by drawing together a small fold of material, then stitching flat.

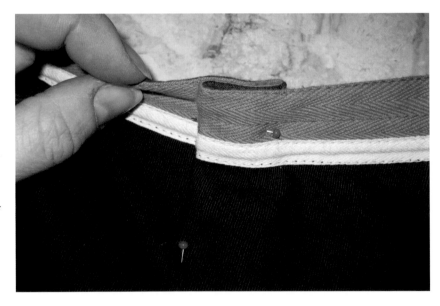

STEP 6

Stitch the back cross-straps securely in place at an angle of approximately 45° from the central seam. Position the front cross-straps so their uppermost end is on the neckline directly below where the diagonal piece of trim joins the edge. The short strap should be on the left side of the rug and will be approximately 18 in (45 cm) in length; the long strap is on the other side and will be approximately 64 in (162.5 cm). Stitch the straps securely in place.

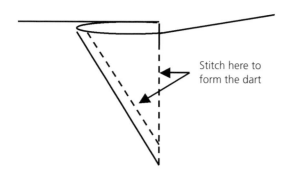

Stitch here to form the dart

STEP 7

Pin the binding in place to edge the outside perimeter of the rug, starting from the centre of the back seam and pinning it to the right side (outside) of the material, leaving approximately one-third protruding beyond the rug edge. Sew in place, then turn the rug over and fold the binding down (it can help to iron it), then sew in place.

STEP 8

Make two loops for the filet string as described in Turning a Duvet Into a Rug, step eight and sew to the inside of the back of the rug. Next, attach either one or two fastenings to the front of the rug over the reinforced material.

Cross-straps and buckles

Fastenings and straps need to be of sufficient quality and strength to hold up to the job, and garment or dress fittings are not suitable. Straps, which can be used for cross-straps or for fastenings at the front of the rug, should be strong webbing or canvas and can be purchased from 'outward bound' shops, occasionally from haberdashers and upholsterers, direct from saddlers or saddlery shops and on the internet. One site in particular that stocks a wide range of straps and buckles is www.acesupplies.com. Cross-straps should be at least 1½ in (3.8 cm) wide and front-fastening straps at least 1 in (2.5 cm). Leather straps can be used for front fasteners, but realistically by the time you have purchased the equipment necessary to punch and cut the leather and stitch it together, you are better off opting for canvas webbing.

Hints about straps

- To prevent fraying when cutting nylon webbing, pass the cut end over a flame, carefully!

Tip

To prevent cross-straps rubbing, thread them through bicycle inner tubing.

- To punch holes into nylon webbing heat a nail (holding it with pliers) under a flame and punch through.

- When attaching front-fastening straps, position the straps approximately 2 in (5 cm) below the neckline of the rug. The strap that has the buckle attached should be positioned so that the buckle rests approximately 2 in (5 cm) from the outside edge of the rug. This means that when the buckle is fastened it will lie on the rug material and not the horse, where it might rub.

- The other strap should be stitched in line with the buckle strap and on the opposite side of the rug. Stitch this strap on in the same manner and allow approximately 2 in (5 cm) between the stitched section and the front of the rug.

- Cross-straps should be positioned on the diagonal so that the straps cross under the belly. Stitch them securely using a rectangular course with two diagonal rows of stitches to provide a really solid attachment.

- Never throw anything away! Always salvage buckles and useable straps off old rugs, headcollars and equipment, and try to re-use.

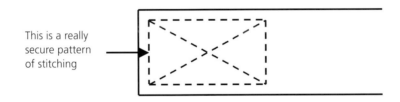

This is a really secure pattern of stitching

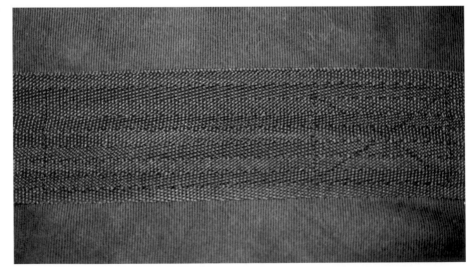

A 'real life' version of the stitching pattern in the diagram.

Making rugs from scratch

As with converting duvets etc., into rugs, the steps for making rugs from scratch are very similar, with changes made primarily in the materials used, the extent of trim or binding, and the configuration of straps and fastenings.

How to make a summer sheet

Summer sheets are possibly one of the most useful rugs around. They can be used in the winter as under-blankets, providing extra layers and warmth under a quilted rug or turnout rug, in the summer for keeping the dust and flies off the stabled horse, or for travelling. By changing the trim on existing sheets, or adding initials or emblems, they can be greatly enhanced and look really smart. Alternatively you can make your own. Again a word of caution; do price-check to find out the cost of buying one. Occasionally with sales and discontinued lines it is possible to pick one up for almost the same price as buying the material and making it yourself.

YOU WILL NEED

Good quality cotton, quantity will vary dependent on size of rug – for a 6 ft 6 in
   (2 m) rug two pieces 37 x 78 in (94 cm x 2 m) (extra width to allow for top seam)
Brightly coloured binding, for a 6 ft 6 in (2 m) rug, 34 ft (10.4 m) of binding
Two pieces of heavier cotton or cotton twill fabric
Strap and buckle or alternative fastening
Cross-straps and fastenings if required
Filet string

STEP 1

Either take measurements for the rug using the method described at the start of this chapter or use an existing rug as a template. You can either make a template from the rug out of newspaper taped together or simply lay the rug over your cotton material and trace around the outside. When cutting the material leave approximately a 1 in (2.5 cm) margin above your marked line along the top edge; this is to allow material to make the seam that joins the two pieces together. Do this twice and cut out the fabric. You now have two pieces of rug-shaped fabric.

STEP 2

Pin the two halves of the rug together and carefully try on the horse to make sure the top seam is lying correctly. Make any adjustments necessary. Stitch the two pieces together along the top seam. Next, open the rug out and fold the two seams down, pin and stitch. If you wish, you can next take two pieces of binding 18 in (45 cm) long and position them onto the central seam 12 in (30 cm) back from the front of the rug. Position them diagonally so they join the front of the rug along the neckline and stitch in place. (These are decorative only and many rugs do not have them.) *See photos below*

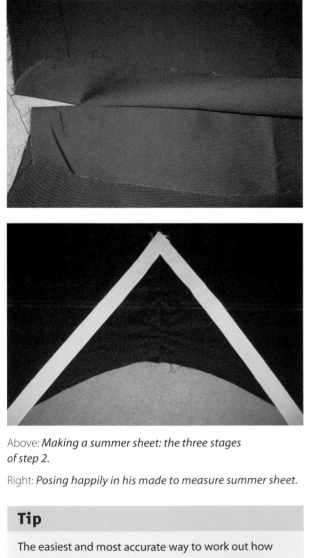

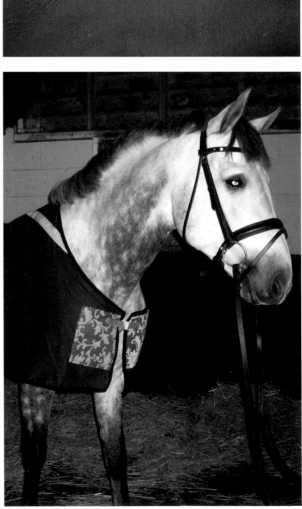

Above: *Making a summer sheet: the three stages of step 2.*

Right: *Posing happily in his made to measure summer sheet.*

Tip

The easiest and most accurate way to work out how much binding is required is to take a measurement off an existing rug. Alternatively, use the following:
3 x length of rug + 4 x depth of rug + 36 in (91 cm) = total amount of binding (generally this works out quite generously, but excess trim can always be used up!)

STEP 3

Next, if you have decided to use cross-straps, position the back cross-straps with their uppermost ends on the central seam. The short strap, approximately 30 in (76 cm) long, should be on the left side of the rug, the long strap, approximately 72 in (183 cm) in length should be on the right side.

STEP 4

Take a 57 in (145 cm) piece of trim and pin over the central seam, the ends of the two 18 in (45 cm) pieces, and the ends of the two back cross-straps. Stitch down securely.

STEP 5

Take the two pieces of heavier cotton material and stitch on the inside shoulder area of the rug – these will bolster up the rug in the area where the fastenings are attached. If you are using decorative material, stitch the shoulder sections on the exterior of the rug and make a feature out of them. Another option is to use the material left over from cutting out the neck section of the rug and stitch this in place instead.

STEP 6

Stitch the back cross-straps securely in place at an angle of approximately 45° from the central seam. Position the front cross-straps so their uppermost ends are on the neckline directly below where the diagonal piece of trim joins the edge. The short strap should be on the left side of the rug and will be approximately 18 in (45 cm) long; the long strap is on the other side and will be approximately 64 in (162.5 cm) in length. Stitch the straps securely in place.

STEP 7

Pin the binding in place to edge the outside perimeter of the rug, starting from the centre of the back seam. It can help to iron the binding in half first, then place over the material edge, pin in place and stitch.

STEP 8

Make two loops for the filet string as described in Turning a Duvet into a Rug, step eight, and sew to the inside of the back of the rug. Next, attach either one or two fastenings to the front of the rug over the reinforced material. *See photos overleaf* ▶

Making a summer sheet.
Above: *Steps 4*
Above right: *Step 5*
Right: *Step 7*

Coolers

Coolers are an extremely popular and useful type of rug. Traditionally they were made from wool, although with new developments in material technology the woollen cooler has been largely replaced by the 'fleece' or similar synthetic fabric. Both woollen coolers and synthetic ones work along the same principle, which is that they wick moisture away from the horse and through to the top of the rug, where it then evaporates. Wool coolers are still very effective and easy to make. Their only real drawback is that they are bulky to wash and dry, and do not wash as easily as synthetic fabrics. Woollen coolers can be made from old wool bed blankets, as described earlier. If making a synthetic fleece or cooler, first do a price-check to ensure that you are saving money by buying the material and making it yourself. Standard fleece material can be bought from many haberdashers or through the internet, although be aware that the more advanced synthetic materials which many of the more expensive coolers are made from are not readily available to buy.

To make coolers follow the same steps as outlined under How to Make a Summer Sheet.

Sweat rugs

Sweat rugs have, to a large extent, been replaced by coolers. The open-weave sweat rug is only effective if used beneath another rug, and can also be used with a layer of straw underneath to increase the wicking away of moisture from the horse. Closed-weave sweat rugs have more of an absorbent action so they are useful for initially putting on a really wet horse after a bath or wash down. However their actual wicking properties are not as good as the cooler system so, once excess water has been absorbed, the rug should be removed and a cooler then used to help dry the horse off without chilling.

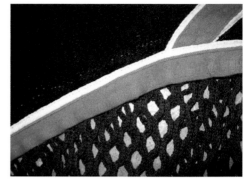

An open-weave sweat rug used under another blanket.

To make sweat rugs follow the same steps as outlined under How to Make a Summer Sheet. Some sweat rugs come without cross-straps, which is fine. However in general a rug with cross-straps is more secure and prevents having to use a roller or surcingle.

Slinkies

Slinkies, sometimes called sleazies or stretch head, neck and shoulder or body covers are excellent rugs made from a stretchy Lycra, elastane, nylon combination. They are tight-fitting and generally used beneath another rug to keep the horse clean and dust-free. Slinkies come in three different formats; full body, head and neck, or shoulders. It is easier to buy these items than to make them, unless you are a skilled seamstress. The material is particularly difficult to work with because of the stretch involved and the fit for the head and neck must be absolutely spot-on to prevent any danger of accident. My advice is to shop for slinkies on eBay or price-check other internet sites, where it is normally possible to buy them for less than the cost of buying the material, and the time involved in making them.

How to stop rugs rubbing

Darts

Altering the fit of the rug is one of the best ways to stop it rubbing. Generally, rubs occur over the shoulders and at the front of the rug. To alter the fit of the rug in this area to make it snugger and more conforming, add one or even two darts to the neckline. Always make the dart on the outside of the rug to prevent a pressure point and further rub! Make a tuck and fold the material over on itself then stitch flat. Sometimes inserting darts to the back edge of the rug can help to improve the fit, especially if the horse has excessively rounded quarters.

Synthetic sheepskin stitched to the inside of a rug can prevent rubbing.

Sheepskin

Sometimes rugs will rub over the area of the withers, particularly if the horse has very pronounced withers. Stitch a piece of synthetic sheepskin to the inside of the rug to cover the withers area – use synthetic sheepskin because it washes more easily, and is less expensive than real sheepskin. The shoulder areas can also be a problem for rubbing, especially during the winter when the stabled horse is rugged most of the time. Cut out two large sections of synthetic sheepskin and stitch to the inside of the rug to cover the problem area.

Shoulder guards

These are made from Lycra, elastane and nylon combinations and are useful for protecting the shoulder area. As mentioned under Slinkies, it is easier and more cost-effective for most people to buy these rather than make them.

Pads

Stitch a foam pad to either side of the withers section. This will help to lift the rug and cut down on rubbing over the withers and shoulders.

'Blinging up' rugs

It is always fun to have rugs with a bit of 'bling', particularly for travelling rugs or rugs used at shows when you are out and about with your horse. It doesn't need to cost a fortune to tart up existing rugs, and old rugs can be transformed relatively quickly and easily.

Trim

Often the trim on rugs starts to show wear and tear first. Change the trim and stitch in place a new, brightly coloured trim. For a really showy look, if

Common sense

If making your own rugs use only good quality and soft fabrics; look for the same in shop-bought items and keep rugs clean, washed and dry.

you have the time, stitch two different trims one behind the other to give a two-tone effect. Using a wider trim than normal can also pep-up a rug and draw attention to it, so opt for a 2 in (5 cm) or wider trim.

It's always fun to have rugs with a bit of 'bling'.

Initials or logo

Personalising rugs is a great way to smarten them up. Large felt initials can be bought from some haberdashers, but it is also very easy to make your own. Make a template out of paper or light card and place over a piece of felt, cut out and stitch on. Initials look best when stitched to the back lower corner of a rug, on either one or both sides. You can also add a 'logo' such as a shamrock leaf, for example, or even a breed brand. Again make a template and place over a piece of felt or coloured material, cut out (hem if necessary) and stitch on. For a really over-the-top look stitch diamante or rhinestone beads to the logo or initials, but be aware that extra care will need to be taken when cleaning the rug.

Shoulder patches

Carefully remove the front fastenings from the rug. Then choose some attractive fabric (cut-offs from furniture fabrics can look really effective) and cut out two segment sections. Place one on either side of the front top corners of the rug and stitch on, remembering to fold under the outer edge, then re-attach the front fastenings.

Above: *There are plenty of suitable fabrics to choose from.*

Above right: *Stitching the fabric.*

Right: *The finished product.*

Protective clothing

Travelling bandages

I prefer to travel using bandages rather than travelling boots. Although travelling boots have greatly improved in design, they are still notorious for slipping and coming undone. It is possible to make your own travelling boots, but they can be bought for virtually the same cost as making them, plus factoring in the time element involved. Travelling bandages are really easy to make as well as being very economical. Often shop-bought bandages can be frustratingly short; they need to be at least 7 ft 6 in (2.3 m) long, and I prefer 8–10 ft (2.4–3 m) bandages.

The width of the bandage is up to you, but a suitable width is between 4 and 5 in (10–12.5 cm). Dependent on the width of the material being used it is possible to get all four bandages (and sometimes more) from one stretch. Bear in mind too, that left-over material can be used for other items such as tail bags.

YOU WILL NEED

A length of material of suitable weight, i.e., fleece or wool (old woollen bed blankets can be used)

13 ft of ½ in wide (4 m of 1.25 cm) cotton tape or 20 in (50 cm) of heavyweight Velcro

Sharp scissors

Ruler and a marker pen or a chalk line

STEP **1**

Lay the material flat and mark out the four divisions, then carefully cut out the four bandage strips. A chalk line can be used to draw the lines along which to cut, but this requires another person to hold one end!

STEP **2**

At one end of each strip fold the two sides together to form a triangle and stitch together.

STEP **3**

Cut the tape into four. Take each piece and place along the central seam on the pointed end of the bandage. Then stitch along the seam to secure, leaving approximately the same length of tape free at either end. If using Velcro, then turn the bandage over so that the seamed side at the pointed end is seam down. Cut the Velcro into four pieces and separate the top from the bottom. Take one top piece and sew the top of the pointed end, leaving approximately 4 in (10 cm) projecting. Then stitch the bottom piece of the Velcro on the same side of the bandage, approximately 5 in (12.5 cm) from the top piece. *See photos overleaf* ▶

Bandage pads

Bandage pads can be made easily, and to the precise length you require – all too often shop-bought pads never quite seem to be the right length. Simple cotton quilted fabric can be bought from most haberdashers or from the internet and is very inexpensive to buy. Measure the length that you require based on allowing enough padding to extend slightly up above the top of

> **Tip**
>
> Hem both ends of your tape first so it doesn't fray.

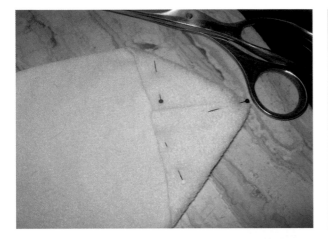

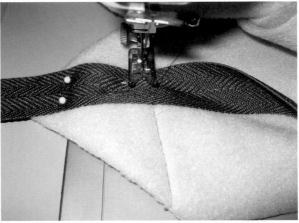

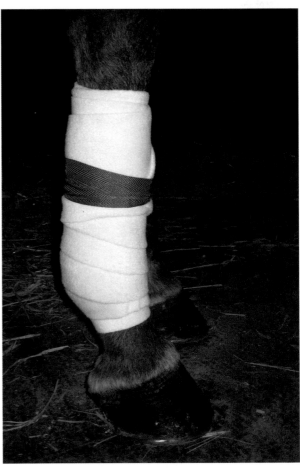

Making travelling bandages.

Top row and above: *steps 2 and 3.*

Right: *The finished bandage in place.*

Tip

Before sewing the bottom piece of Velcro on, put the bandage on the horse and double-check to see where the bottom piece of Velcro needs to sit. It will vary according to the amount of bone the horse has and the type of padding used underneath.

the bandage, and well down below the bandage to cover the heel bulbs and coronary band.

YOU WILL NEED

Cotton quilted fabric – for a 16 hh horse back pads
   need to be at least 24 x 16½ in (61 cm x 42 cm)
   and front pads need to be at least 24 x 14½ in
   (61 x 37 cm)
1½ or 2 in (3.8 or 5 cm) wide binding to trim the edges

STEP **1**

Measure and cut out the piece of material of the right size for the front and hind pads.

STEP **2**

Starting in the middle of the short side, pin the trim all the way around the pad so that approximately one-third of it projects beyond the edge of the material, then stitch it in place.

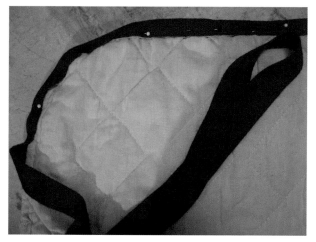

A homemade bandage pad.

STEP **3**

Fold the trim down over the other side of the material and pin in place (it can be helpful to iron it over). Then stitch in place.

Simple poll protector

These can be useful, especially when travelling very large horses that run the risk of bashing their heads. Neither one of the types described look very pretty but they are very cheap and effective.

Pattern one

YOU WILL NEED

Either an old leather browband or a piece of webbing 1 in (2.5 cm) wide and
   approximately 20 in (50 cm) long
A piece of foam at least 3 in (7.5 cm) thick: you will need to measure the length you
   need according to the horse

STEP **1**

Make two parallel slots with a sharp knife through the top end and bottom end of the foam.

STEP **2**

Slide one end of the browband onto the headcollar and thread the other end through one of the pair of slots in the foam. If you do not have an old browband, then take the webbing and measure the correct length against the horse. Turn over each end and sew across to leave a loop. You now have a 'custom made' browband.

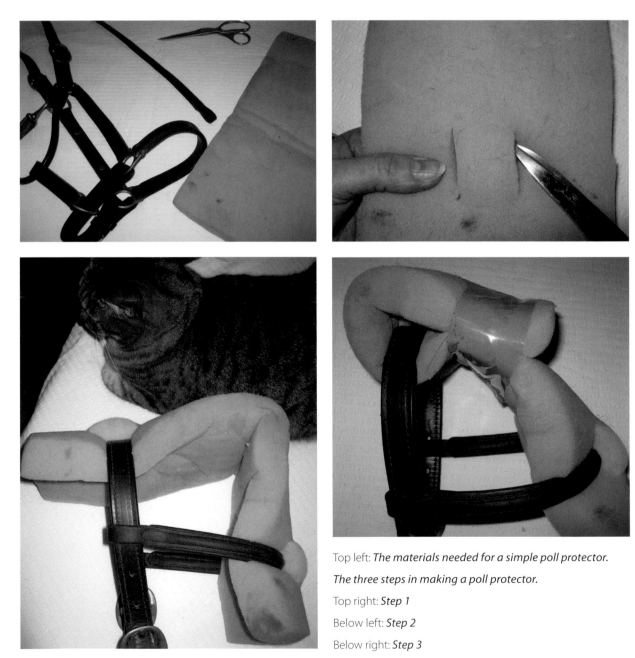

Top left: *The materials needed for a simple poll protector.*

The three steps in making a poll protector.

Top right: *Step 1*

Below left: *Step 2*

Below right: *Step 3*

STEP 3

Slide the headcollar strap through the top piece of the foam, and then attach the other end of the browband to the headcollar.

NB: for added protection to the poll area, take the end of your foam strip and double it back over the top of the headcollar, then staple or tape in place.

Pattern two

Another simple way to protect the poll is to buy a piece of pipe insulation from a hardware shop or plumbing supplier, and thread the top of the headcollar through it. Once it is on the headcollar, fasten the insulation by wrapping electrical tape around it. This won't win any fashion awards, but is a quick, easy and cheap way to protect the poll.

Anti-rubbing cuffs

Headcollars in particular can cause rubbing on thin-skinned horses, and lining the headcollar with synthetic sheepskin can help to cut down on this. Ideally you want to make sheepskin cuffs that are removable so they can be washed and also transferred to a different headcollar if necessary.

YOU WILL NEED

Synthetic sheepskin cut into strips to the length of the parts of the headcollar to be covered, and wide enough to wrap around the piece and provide room to attach Velcro for fastening

Enough narrow (approximately 0.5 in/1.25 cm) Velcro dependent on how many cuffs you need to make

STEP 1

Measure the lengths of sheepskin required against the headcollar (i.e., to cover the front of the noseband and/or the cheekpieces and/or the headpiece and cut to size.

STEP 2

Stitch a length of Velcro to each cuff. Stitch the top piece of Velcro to the underside of the top of the cuff, and the bottom piece of the Velcro to the outer edge of the bottom part of cuff.

Fly fringes

There are several different ways to make a fly fringe, but a couple of the easiest are as follows.

Pattern one

YOU WILL NEED

Either an old browband, or a piece of 1 in (2.5 cm) wide webbing/canvas
approximately 20 in (50 cm) long
A quantity of baling twine
A hole punch, or a sharp nail

STEP 1

If using an old browband, take the hole punch and punch a series of small holes across the front of the leather leaving approximately ½ in (1.25 cm) in between. If you do not have a spare browband then take a piece of webbing/canvas around 20 in (50 cm) in length (dependent on the size of the horse). Fold 2 in (5 cm) at both ends of the webbing back on itself and stitch to form a loop at either end. You should now have a webbing browband that measures 16 in (40.5 cm). Heat a sharp nail, holding it with pliers and punch holes across the front of the webbing.

STEP 2

Take the baling twine and cut into lengths of approximately 1 ft (30 cm). Starting with the first hole, thread the twine through from the back to the front. Tie a double knot in the end and pull the length tight so it dangles down from the browband. Repeat all the way along. If you have the time you can plait your lengths of twine before threading through the hole, to make a more robust fly fringe.

Pattern two

YOU WILL NEED

An old browband or a piece of 1 in (2.5 cm) wide webbing/canvas approximately
20 in (50 cm) long
A piece of soft, thin leather, or an old chammy leather approximately 12 in (30 cm)
long by 14 in (35.5 cm) wide

STEP **1**

If you do not have a browband to use then make one out of the webbing as outlined above. Turn the top of the piece of leather/chammy back on itself by approximately 1½–2 in (3.8–5 cm) and stitch along the bottom edge.

STEP **2**

Take a sharp pair of scissors and cut vertically upwards across the leather to form a number of tassels.

STEP **3**

Thread the browband through the top of the leather.

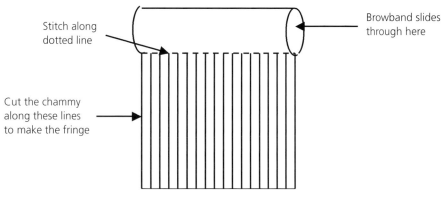

Making a browband, pattern two.

Tail guards

Tails are especially vulnerable when the horse is travelling, and the use of tail guards can make all the difference. There are a number of different approaches for making tail guards. A couple of the simplest are as follows.

Pattern one

YOU WILL NEED

A piece of thick foam approximately 2 in (5 cm) thickness that measures 16 x 8 in (40.5 x 20 cm)

Two tail bandages

STEP **1**

Bandage the tail as normal starting from the dock and working down to the end of the tailbone.

STEP 2

Position the foam over the tailbone so that it extends approximately 2 in (5 cm) above the dock and covers the top section of tailbone.

STEP 3

Take the second bandage and, starting at the top, bandage the tail to secure the foam.

Pattern two

YOU WILL NEED

Two pieces of cotton or fleece material 16 x 12 in (40.5 x 30 cm)
One piece of either ¼ in (0.5 cm) thick foam measuring 16 x 12 in (40.5 x 30 cm) or a
    piece of quilted material of the same measurement
21 ft (6.4 m) of 1 in (2.5 cm) wide trim for binding

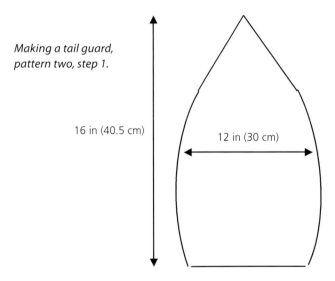

Making a tail guard, pattern two, step 1.

16 in (40.5 cm)

12 in (30 cm)

STEP 1

It is possible to use the leftover material from cutting out a rug pattern to make a tail guard. Cut out the two pieces of material and the foam, following the pattern in the first diagram. Then place the foam or quilting in between the other two pieces and stitch all three together.

STEP 2

Measure the trim to go around the perimeter of the tail guard, cut and then iron it in half along its length. Place so it fits over the outside edge of the guard and stitch in place. Next cut three 3 ft (91 cm) lengths of trim and stitch onto the outside of the guard where indicated on the pattern.

STEP **3**

Take the remaining trim and fold in half, ironing the crease. Then fold each half back again by 1 in (2.5 cm) and iron. You should now have a pyramid shaped fold. Place this over the pointed end of the guard with the loose ends of the trim pointing away from the guard, and stitch securely in place using a rectangular pattern with crossed diagonals in the middle.

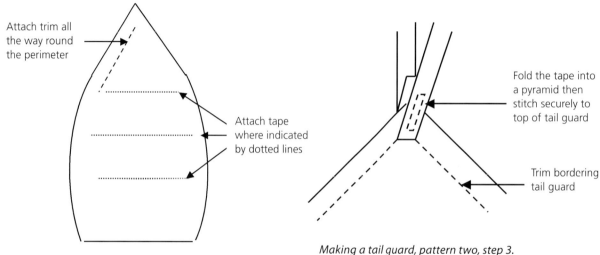

Attach trim all the way round the perimeter

Attach tape where indicated by dotted lines

Fold the tape into a pyramid then stitch securely to top of tail guard

Trim bordering tail guard

Making a tail guard, pattern two, step 3.

Making a tail guard, pattern two, step 2.

Tail bags

These are useful for protecting the long tail hairs and are frequently used in the US particularly on stable-kept horses. The ends of the tail are very vulnerable and can be dry, become brittle and break off easily, especially when the horse is swishing its tail during the summer. Tail bags should be used with caution and should be regularly removed (twice daily) and put back on. Do not make them too long otherwise the horse may step on them and cause further damage to the tail.

There are two types of tail bag, a single bag and a series of three bags fastened together. In each instance the bottom of the bag is open to allow you to thread the tail hairs through; they can then be closed with a rubber band.

Before putting a tail bag on, either braid the tail hairs into one single braid for the single bag, or into three bunches for the multiple bag.

Above: *A tail bag secured correctly.*

Left: *Tail bags are useful for protecting the long tail hairs.*

Never secure tail bags by wrapping the ties around the tailbone, as this can restrict the circulation and lead to severe problems. Instead lace the ties through the top of your braid/s.

Single bag

YOU WILL NEED

Fleece material long enough to measure from the bottom of the tailbone to
  cover the ends of the tail hair: this will vary from horse to horse – the sample bag
  is 43 x 12½ in (110 x 32 cm) long and is suitable for a 16 hh horse
30 in of 1 in or ½ in (76 cm of 2.5 cm or 1.25 cm) tape
Needle, thread

STEP **1**
Hem the bottom end of your piece of material.

STEP 2

Hem the top end, then fold over by ½ in (1.25 cm) and stitch along the bottom. The tape will be threaded through here.

STEP 3

Turn the material so the right sides are facing each other and sew down the long edge to join them. Start sewing below the hem loop you have left to thread the tape through.

STEP 4

Hem the ends of your tape then, using a safety pin, thread the tape through the open hem.

The bag is now ready to use.

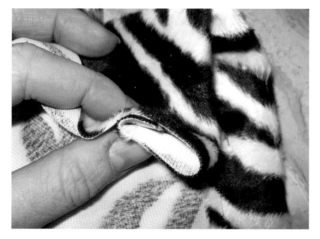

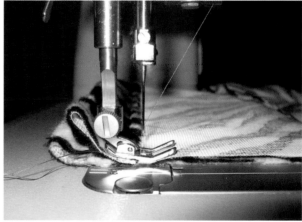

Making a tail bag.

Above left: *Step 2*

Above right: *Step 3*

Left: *Step 4*

Multiple bag

With the multiple bag, divide the hair into three bunches then thread each bunch through one of the bags. Then braid the bags together and fasten the end with a rubber band.

YOU WILL NEED

Again you will need fleece material long enough to measure from the bottom of the tailbone to cover the ends of the tail hair: this will vary from horse to horse – the sample bag is 43 x 12 in (110 cm x 30 cm) long and is suitable for a 16 hh horse

36 in of 1 in or ½ in (91 cm of 2.5 cm or 1.25 cm) tape

Needle, thread

STEP 1

Measure and cut out the three pieces of fleece and hem exactly the same way as described for the single bag.

STEP 2

Turn the material so the right sides are facing each other and sew down the long edge to join them. Start sewing below the hem loop you have left to thread the tape through.

STEP 3

Hem the ends of the tape then thread through the top of each bag using a safety pin.

The bag is now ready to use.

Above and left: *Making a multiple bag, steps 1, 2 and 3.*

Browbands

Browbands are one item of horse apparel that can really catch the eye. 'Bling' is definitely the order of the day, but often it doesn't come cheap. There are quite a few companies that now specialise in custom-making 'bling' browbands, but they are expensive, and often over the top. The secret with 'bling' is finding the balance between an elegant statement and a garish disaster. Subtlety should, in most cases, be the first consideration. Also avoid using a hugely decorative browband on a very lightweight, fine show pony or small-headed horse. There is always a danger of the browband eclipsing the horse altogether. Try to match the right amount of 'bling' not only to the size, character and weight of the horse, but also to the class the horse is being shown in. Generally it is best to keep 'bling' browbands for best because the decorative details will not always stand up to everyday use.

Browbands are items that can really catch the eye.

How to make velvet- or silk-covered browbands

The traditional type of show browband is covered in velvet or silk. Covering your own is relatively simple to do and fairly cost-effective. The main advantage is that you can then chose the exact colours you want to use, and match them into the rest of your outfit and turnout. There are several different patterns of velvet- or silk-covered browband.

Pattern one – shark's teeth design

YOU WILL NEED

An old leather browband (make sure the stitching, etc. is sound)
Two lengths of either velvet or silk ribbon that is the same width as the browband
    and three times its length
Needle and thread

*Materials needed for a
shark's teeth browband.*

*Making a shark's teeth
browband, step 1.*

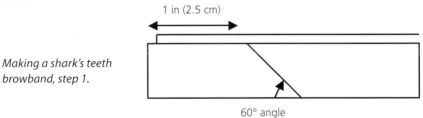

1 in (2.5 cm)

60° angle

STEP **1**

Place the two pieces of ribbon one on top of the other with the velvet side facing outwards. Approximately 1 in (2.5 cm) from one end sew the two pieces together at an angle of 60°.

STEP **2**

Place the browband between the two pieces of ribbon (A and B) with the outside aspect of it facing you.

STEP **3**

Fold A over and down between piece B and the browband, then fold piece B over, down, under and up. It should cover A at the front and then pass between A and the browband at the back.

STEP **4**

Next fold A under, up, over and down, so it covers piece B at the front and passes between it and the browband at the back.

STEP **5**

Continue to thread the two pieces over each other until the end of the browband, then stitch the two together and trim the ends. It can be helpful to put a dab of clear nail varnish on the ends to cut down on fraying.

Making a shark's teeth browband.

Step 2

Step 4

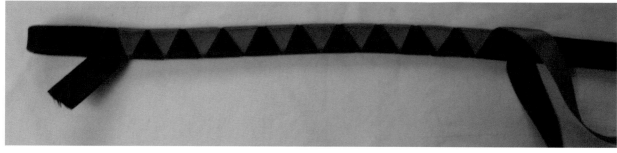

Above and below: *Step 5*

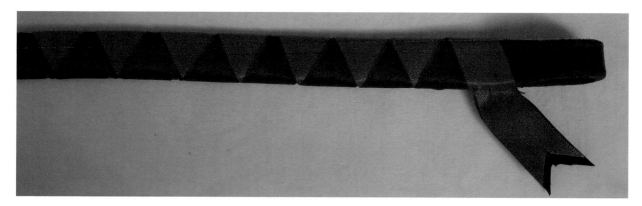

Pattern two – three-coloured design

YOU WILL NEED

An old browband (with sound stitching)

One length of velvet or silk ribbon the same width as the browband and three times as long (piece A)

Two lengths of different coloured velvet or silk ribbon half the width of the browband and three times its length (piece B and C)

Needle and thread

STEP 1

Lay piece A flat with the velvet side (or shiny side) down, then lay the two half-width pieces, B and C, on top of it with the velvet facing up, and next to each other (see photo). Approximately 1 in (2.5 cm) from the end sew all three pieces together with a single row of stitching at 60°.

STEP 2

Place the browband with the outside edge facing you between piece A and pieces B and C, so that pieces B and C are facing you. Fold pieces B and C down and over to pass between the browband and piece A.

STEP 3

Fold piece A over, down, under and up. It should cover pieces B and C at the front and pass between them and the browband at the back.

STEP 4

Fold pieces B and C under, up, over and down to cover piece A at the front and to pass between the browband and piece A at the back.

STEP 5

Continue in this manner until the end of the browband. Stitch the three pieces together and trim the ends of the ribbon. Use a dab of clear nail varnish to help stop fraying.

See photos opposite ▶

Opposite page: *Making a three-coloured browband.*

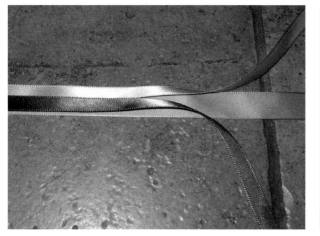

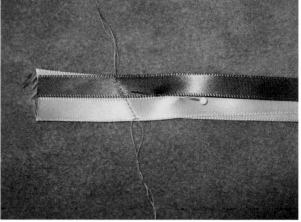

Top row: *Step 1*

Middle row: *Step 2*

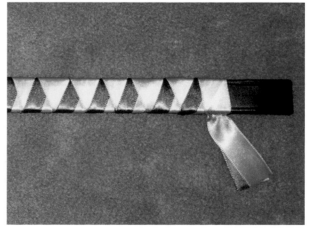

Step 4

Step 5

Pattern three – diamond pattern

YOU WILL NEED

An old browband (make sure the stitching is sound)

One piece of velvet or silk ribbon, slightly wider than the browband and five times its length in one colour

One piece of velvet or silk ribbon, slightly wider than the browband and five times its length in a different colour

Needle and thread

Tip

Label your four pieces with a small piece of paper stuck on with tape at the bottom to avoid confusion.
Also secure the top as seen in the photo showing step three.

STEP 1

Cut each piece of ribbon in half. You should now have four pieces the same length, piece A and C in one colour and piece B and D in another. Lay piece A velvet side down and on top of it lay piece B velvet side up then stitch them together approximately 1 in (2.5 cm) from the end and at a 45° angle. Repeat with the other two pieces C and D. (Pieces A and D are the same colour; in the photo sequence they are lilac, pieces B and C are green.)

STEP 2

Hold the browband vertically and insert between the first pair of C and D ribbons, see photo. Then place the second pair of A and B ribbons as seen in the photo. The colour to appear as the diamond should be lying on the outside of the front and the back of the browband (in the photo, this is the lilac).

STEP 3

Pass piece A (lilac) round to the back of the browband and underneath green B. Pass piece D (lilac) round to the front underneath green piece C.

STEP 4

Next, pass piece B (green) over the front and underneath piece D (lilac). Then piece C (green) comes across the back and underneath piece A (lilac).

Tip

This is quite a difficult pattern to follow and is a case of trial and error and persevering! It will eventually become clear!

STEP 5

Now take piece D (lilac) and pass it round the back and under piece C (green).
Next piece A (lilac) comes across the front and under piece B (green).

STEP 6

Then pass piece C (green) over the front and underneath piece A (lilac). Next piece B (green) comes round the back and under piece C (lilac). Repeat these steps until you reach the end of the browband.

STEP 7

Turn the browband horizontally and fold the ends of the ribbon down and then stitch all four pieces together on each end. Trim the ends and seal with clear nail varnish.

Making a diamond pattern browband.

Top row: *Step 1*

Middle row, left: *Step 2*

Middle row, right: *Step 3*

Left: *Step 5*

How to make browband rosettes

For a little extra pizzazz try adding a rosette to each end of the browband. Again, if doing this, make sure that the size of the rosette does not overpower the browband and the horse. These can be quite fiddly to make at first, but once you get the hang of them they are fun and easy to do.

YOU WILL NEED

Several different coloured pieces of ribbon; the width and length will depend on the size of the rosette you make

A piece of lightweight card

Glue (glue guns are good, or a regular strong, binding glue)

Sharp scissors

A decorative button or bead

STEP 1

Determine the size of rosette you wish to make and cut a circle out of the cardboard. The actual perimeter of the rosette will be slightly larger than the cardboard circle.

STEP 2

Start with the first colour ribbon for the bottom layer. Cut six pieces of ribbon approximately 2 in (5 cm), though the length will depend on the width of ribbon you are using, for example ribbon that is 1 in (2.5 cm) wide will need to be approximately 2½ in (6.3 cm) long. Lay the ribbon flat then fold the two ends over each other and pull tight to make a cone. Dot some glue to the back flat piece and stick to the card. Continue all the way around the card spacing the six pieces evenly in a star formation.

STEP 3

Choose a different colour ribbon and repeat the process to create a second layer with the points alternating with the bottom layer. Position the second layer further to the centre of the card.

STEP 4

Repeat the process if required with a third, fourth or fifth layer. The final layer can be with a smaller ribbon, in the photo the final layer is ribbon ⅕ in (0.5 cm) wide by 1⅔ in (4 cm) long. Next, take your button, and if it is hollow-backed, fill the back with glue and press down firmly in the centre. If the button has a shank then carefully cut this off with a pair of pliers first before gluing the button.

Tip

To protect fabric and decorated browbands spray with Scotchguard. Clean them very carefully, preferably with a dry cloth or a wrung out damp rag.

STEP **5**

To make the tail for the rosette, combine the ribbons in a short length, stitch together at the top, then glue to the back of the rosette. Trim the ends and fix with clear nail polish. Then glue to the browband.

Making a browband rosette.

Step 1

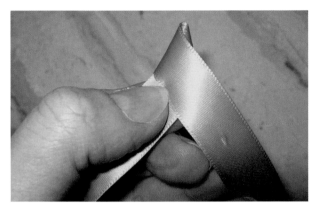

Step 2

Step 2 continued

Step 3

Step 4

Step 5

The rosettes are fairly fragile and the glue will occasionally dry and crack. Always take a tube of glue with you to a show to re-fix any rosettes that might get knocked off, and treat the browband carefully to prolong its life!

Diamante and decorative rivets on browbands

These can look really stunning, though they are reasonably fragile so take care when using them and cleaning them. The most effective way to really 'bling up' browbands is to use decorative rivets. Rivet sets (basically a thick leather pad and a punch) can be bought pretty cheaply, with Tandy Leather Factory UK providing some of the best and most reasonable kits. The disadvantage is their high shipping costs. This company also sells a selection of decorative rivets, which look fantastic on browbands, dog collars and belts. eBay can also be a good source of tools and rivets.

First work out your pattern of rivets then measure the browband to ensure that the rivets are spaced regularly. Punch out a suitable-sized hole using a leather punch, and then insert the rivet using the rivet kit.

Diamante and decorative rivets on browbands can look stunning.

CHAPTER 3

Rider's clothing

Riding kit has become more and more subject to fashion recently, with great emphasis on style and looking good, both on and off the horse. If you have the money it is worth spending it on certain high-quality items as they will last far longer than their cheaper counterparts. Riding jackets and boots, for example, are items worth splashing out on, if possible, because the cut and quality of them is noticeably better, whereas it is possible to get by with a cheaper pair of jodhpurs/breeches and shirts. Try buying more expensive items such as jackets, from eBay, where it is possible to get a real bargain, or revamp older jackets to give them a more modern look. *Riding hats should always be of the highest quality possible and must always conform to the current safety standards. Never buy hats from the internet or mail order. It is essential they fit absolutely correctly and they should be tried on before purchasing.*

There are patterns available for making items such as showing jackets, jodhpurs, even side-saddle habits, shirts, etc. from scratch, and certainly this can be more cost-effective. However making items such as these does require a certain needlecraft skill, and occasionally the time involved in grappling with the patterns and trying to make-do outweighs the cost of purchasing from a cheap, reliable source. Working with existing items and smartening them up or changing their look using simple and cheap methods is an alternative.

Shirts

A primary consideration with riding shirts is for them to fit properly and not feel constrictive, and for them to be breathable. With this in mind avoid nylon shirts if possible, and opt for either cotton, or a cotton/Lycra mix. If looking to purchase new shirts always check for bargain-basement sales and on internet sites, although remember to factor in the cost of postage and packaging. It is not necessary to buy those sold specifically as riding shirts – any white shirts, including school shirts, will work provided they are not too baggy or too tight. In fact, if you are small enough, children's school shirts can be bought very cheaply and do not have VAT added. For larger individuals, plain shirts can still be bought cheaply at some of the supermarkets or cheaper clothes shops. It is also possible to work with shirts that you already have, and to change them or smarten them up, turning them into smart show wear.

Changing buttons

Changing buttons is a great way to instantly perk up shirts and jackets. Change front and cuff buttons, and replace with mother of pearl or even diamante for real 'bling'. Even replacing a normal shirt button with brightly coloured buttons can make a difference; try to match them with the colour of stock or tie that you will be wearing. Some buttons (especially diamante) can be quite expensive, so try to salvage anything from old clothing, or trawl through charity shops to find suitable buttons or even shirts that can be revamped.

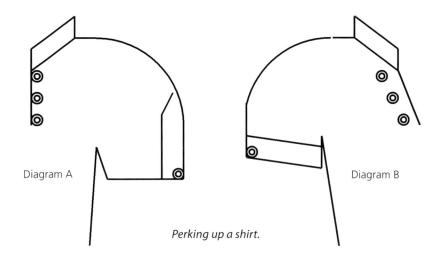

Diagram A   Diagram B

Perking up a shirt.

Short-sleeved shirts are of real benefit for the summer show season. Perk up the sleeves by sewing buttons on the top, see diagram A. You can also stitch a small piece of material, as indicated on the diagram, and then place the button on top of this. A dart of contrasting material such as this can really brighten up an old shirt.

Alternatively, stitch a piece of contrasting material around the bottom of the sleeve as indicated on diagram B, and then place your button on top. Another idea is to cut the shirt material where indicated along the dotted line on diagram B. Hem both sides of the split and then stitch a small button on either side. This is quite an attractive detail for a shirt.

Shirt collars

To really tart up a collar, sew two very small diamante chips, logos, or similar detailing onto the points of the collar. Try to choose something that will match the tie you will be wearing. The trick is to keep it small and unobtrusive so it lends glamour without being over the top.

Trims and logos

Trim

Adding trim to shirts and to jackets can make a big difference.

YOU WILL NEED

An old patterned shirt, or material fragments that can be bought very cheaply from haberdashers
Needle, thread, pins and scissors

STEP **1**
Trim can be added in different places; personally I think it looks really smart when a contrasting piece of material is added to the cuffs of the shirt, across the top of the pocket and over the shoulders, but any or all of these can be done at your discretion. Measure the amount of material necessary for the part you are trimming.

STEP **2**
Cut the material out and hem, then pin to the shirt.

STEP **3**
Stitch onto the shirt. When doing this be sure that the material you are adding to the shirt will not run its colours when washed!!

Sometimes just adding a small band of material to the shirt cuffs can be enough to perk it up.

Logos

Applying logos or patterns to a shirt can personalise it and make it more glamorous. Large patterns, such as a star for example, or four-leafed clover, can be added to the back of the shirt. This will not show when your jacket is on, but when you take your jacket off suddenly you appear in a really original shirt. This can also be done to your regular riding clothes and T-shirts to pep them up. Choose a suitable material, preferably one that is similar to the shirt's material. Draw out your logo or pattern on the reverse of the material, cut out, hem and stitch to the shirt. (It is not always necessary to hem, although preferable. If deciding not to hem, try to choose a material that is resistant to fraying, and then stitch on using a zigzag stitch across the edge of the material.)

Smaller logos or patterns can be added to the pocket area on the front of shirts. Make sure they are positioned so that they will not be seen when a show jacket is on. The top of short sleeves on the shirt can also be treated in this way.

Star patterns added to a shirt to personalise it.

Jackets

Jackets, including showing, hacking, hunting, dressage and side-saddle, can be seriously expensive to buy, although generally (and provided one's shape does not change too much), once bought they will last for a long time. With jackets, fit is of supreme importance. They must fit well to give an elegant appearance, but also be comfortable to ride in and non-restrictive. With hunt coats, it's useful if they have big pockets!

For the ambitious or experienced seamstress, jackets can be made, and patterns are available on the internet or from good dress shops. For everyone else, reasonably priced jackets can be purchased from a variety of sources. They are often included in end-of or mid-season sales, so aim to buy only at these times. Second-hand jackets are an option, though it is generally best to view them before purchasing so you are aware of their state of repair. Old jackets and second-hand jackets can be perked up considerably provided the fabric is still in reasonable condition, has not faded and has not worn unduly.

General care and maintenance

To keep jackets looking their best:

- Hang them on padded or shaped coat-hangers (wrapping old nylons around a wire hanger also works).

- Keep them covered, preferably in a cotton bag.

- Keep them out of direct sunlight to prevent fabric fading.

- Keep mothballs or cedar in the pockets, remembering to remove before wearing.

- Before wearing, check buttons to make sure threads are tight.

- Only wear when showing, competing, etc., and at all other times keep stored.

- De-fuzz or de-ball material carefully and, if necessary, paying attention to the elbow area and under the arms.

- Always clean down with a damp cloth or wet wipe before storing.

- Pass a wet wipe over jackets, especially velvet collars immediately prior to entering the show ring to remove any specks of dirt or dust.

- Use clear adhesive tape wrapped around the hand to pull stray horse hairs from the material.

- For any small areas on the jacket that might have worn, particularly the collar, try adding a dab of colour with a marker pen. From a distance it will not show.

Jacket collars

A jacket can be perked up by changing the collar. Dark blue or black jackets can look lovely with a paler coloured collar – either a pale blue, green, lilac or pink looks particularly good. Covering collars is quite tricky to do well, but it is possible to do without removing the existing material. To really add a finishing touch, add a little trim, the same colour as your new collar, across the front pockets.

YOU WILL NEED

A piece of thin, stretchy velvet material approximately 20 x 8 in (50 x 20 cm)
Needle, thread
Paper to make a pattern, and a pencil

STEP **1**

Lay your jacket out with the collar as flat as possible on a table, then lay a piece of large paper underneath the collar and trace the top line of the collar and the angle that it will travel down at. Now measure the length of the two diagonal sides. Remove the jacket and draw in the rest of the pattern. This is not an exact science but is to provide roughly the shape needed. Your pattern should now look similar to the one in the diagram.

STEP **2**

Cut out your material. Then position the jacket so that the collar is in its normal 'wearing' position and position the material to cover it. Start at one end of the collar, pinning the velvet down. This is really fiddly and it's difficult to get all the creases out so that the material lies flat. If you use stretchy velvet you can pull the material tight to remove the creases.

STEP **3**

Now carefully hand-stitch the velvet into place. Don't forget to turn the edges over to hem and to keep the material pulled nice and tight to get rid of creases.

Hacking jackets come in a wide variety of different tweeds, and adding a new velvet collar to these can really make a difference. Try a contrasting darker colour: either a forest green or brown for lighter-coloured jackets, or a paler olive green, ochre or tan for darker jackets.

If you do not wish to re-cover the entire collar, try adding piping around the collar perimeter. This again is quite fiddly to do without unpicking the collar, but it can be done with some patience!

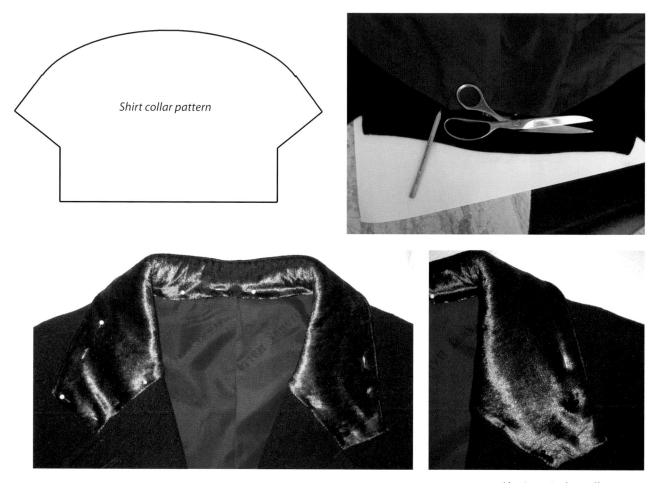

Shirt collar pattern

Altering a jacket collar.
Top right: *Step 1*
Below left: *Step 2*
Below right: *Step 3*

Braid or piping around collars

YOU WILL NEED

40 in (1 m) of ⅙ in (4 mm) wide coloured braid
Needle and thread

STEP 1

A lot of jackets have a seam in their lining running vertically from the middle of the bottom of the collar down the back. Insert the end of your braid into the fold caused by this seam and then stitch down. This is a neat way to start and finish the braid, otherwise you can either unpick a small section of the lining, insert the end of the braid and re-stitch, or stitch the end of the braid to prevent fraying and then start sewing it onto the collar from the inside bottom edge.

STEP **2**

Align the braid so that it is on the very edge of the collar and follow the line of the collar round. Pin in place, then hand-sew on. It can be helpful to tack it on before sewing.

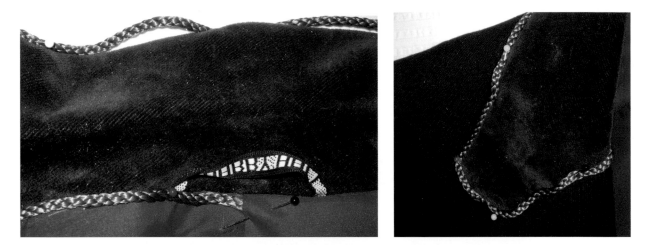

The steps to putting braid on a collar.

Top row: *Steps 1 and 2*

Right: *The edging finished.*

Other features of jackets

Pockets

Add a piece of trim to the pockets in the same colour as the collar. This really gives the jacket definition and a very finished look. Pockets can either have a narrow strip across the top, or a band of piping. Piping looks very effective particularly when the collar has also been piped.

Buttons

As with shirts, changing the buttons on a jacket is a quick and easy way to give it an instant new look. Sometimes buttons in contrasting colours i.e. light-coloured buttons on dark jackets or vice versa can look really good. Don't forget to change the cuff buttons and the two buttons at the back of the jacket (if it has any) as well. Brass buttons can look good on the right jacket – but make sure you keep them shiny!

Jacket back

Some jackets have beautifully tailored backs to them, often with two buttons and a piece of horizontal piping. Change the look of the jacket by changing the buttons and running a new and contrasting piece of piping along the back.

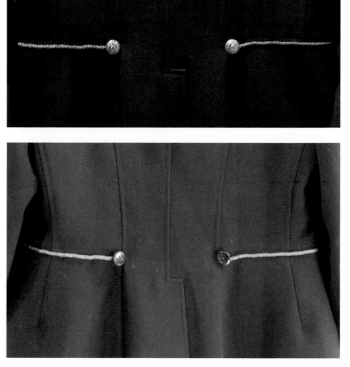

Above: *Changing the buttons can give a jacket a new look.*

Below: *The look of a jacket can be altered by changing the buttons and running contrasting piping along the back.*

Jodhpurs/breeches

It is possible to buy jodhpurs (or breeches, for male riders) pretty cheaply, especially from some of the larger equestrian supply shops, or even some of the large supermarkets. However, cheap jodhpurs are just that, and they will wear old quickly, whereas the more expensive makes are crafted from better quality fabrics and will last much better. However, in terms of cosmetics it is not generally necessary to spend a fortune on jodhpurs or breeches; a cheap pair can look just as good as an expensive pair, even if they do not last as well.

There are various ways to perk jodhpurs up:

- Many jodhpurs today come with small belt loops, and adding a belt to them can really improve the look, especially for general riding with a simple long-sleeved shirt tucked in. Coloured elastic belts can normally be picked up really cheaply from clothes shops. Elastic ones are good because they are comfortable and allow movement. Otherwise imitation leather belts are also cheap, and come in a range of colours.

- For jodhpurs without belt loops, it is easier to make your own and attach them to the waistband. Always use at least four loops with either one in the middle of the back of the waistband, or one either side of the middle at the back. This will prevent the back of the jodhpurs from sagging.

- Small logos can be stitched to the front pockets if the jodhpurs have them, or to the back of the jodhpurs directly below the waistband.

- Sewing a button at the base of the front two belt loops can smarten up a pair of jodhpurs.

- Attaching a small flat charm, such as a horse head, to one of the front belt loops can also add a little pizzazz, although be careful to chose one rounded and flat in design to minimise any chance of injury during a fall.

Stocks

Stocks can vary quite considerably in price, mostly dependent on the fabric. The advantages of making one's own are that you can chose your fabric and colours to match your existing jacket and equipment, and that they are fairly simple to make and cost-effective. It is often possible to buy enough material from which to make a tie or stock from bin ends at large department stores. Material bought like this is extremely cost-effective. If you wish to make a silk tie or stock then the cost will be more, but again silks vary quite considerably in price and it is worth looking on the internet as well as in local shops. (It is possible to make your own ties, but to be honest if you shop around it is cheaper, less time-consuming and easier to buy ties!)

How to make a stock

The easiest way to sort out a pattern is to make one from an existing stock, so if you have access to one, through a friend, etc., then trace your pattern from this. If you do not, you will need to draw a pattern out, and the best way to do it is in three separate pieces.

YOU WILL NEED

A piece of cotton material 20 x 44 in (50 cm x 112 cm)
Paper and pencil to make a pattern
Pen to mark the material
Needle and thread

STEP **1**

It is easiest, though not essential, to make the stock in three pieces. Piece A is the centre, 'collar' piece, piece B is the shorter length and piece C is the longer length. Piece B and C are the same shape, but piece C needs to be 1½ in (3.8 cm) longer. Make your pattern and cut the paper pieces out, then lay them over the material and mark with a pencil. Cut two of each piece and remember to allow a margin for a hem between your pencil line and the cut. You should now have 2 x piece A, 2 x piece B and 2 x piece C.

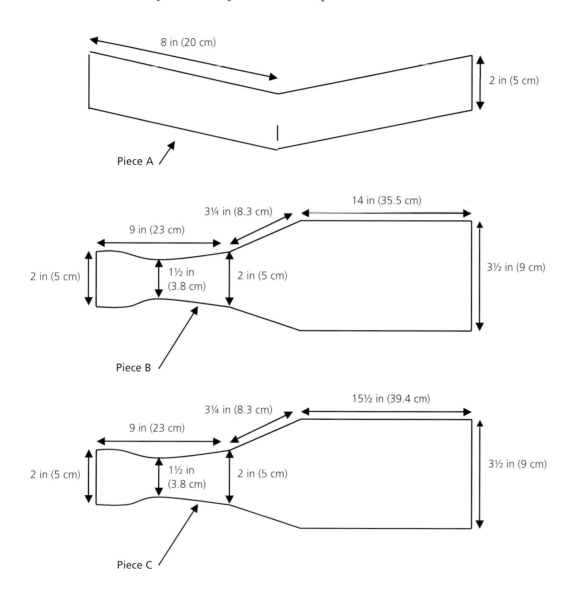

Components and measurements for a stock.

STEP 2

Place the two pieces C with the right side together, pin together and stitch all sides except the short 2 in (5 cm) end. Turn the piece the right way round and carefully iron to flatten the seams. Tuck the end of the open end inside and stitch across the end to seal it. Now place to one side.

STEP 3

Take one piece of B and one piece of A and place with the short ends together (see diagram) then stitch down seam. Do the same with the other two pieces of B and C.

STEP 4

Turn the two attached pieces of A and B right side together and stitch together leaving the short end of pieces A open – the 2 in (5 cm) end. Make sure that the seams from step three line up on both pieces.

STEP 5

Turn the piece the right way out, iron the seams and stitch along the short open end. Next, find the middle of the collar piece (piece A), make a small mark and then make your buttonhole.

STEP 6

Now attach piece C to the other end of the collar piece A using several stout stitches at the top and the bottom, leaving a slot in the middle to pass the stock through when tying it. *See photos opposite* ▶

Stock pins

A stock pin is the finishing touch to a stock and makes all the difference to overall appearance in the ring. The traditional pin is a horizontal one, normally with a decorative feature along its length, or in the middle, but round pins are becoming increasingly popular and can look very polished.

Stock pins can be expensive, though it is possible to buy attractive and reasonable ones from various sites on the internet. However, an even cheaper option is to trawl through second-hand shops for brooches, and provided they are not too big or too 'bling' they can make very good stock pins. Go for narrow horizontal ones, which can be worn either vertically or horizontally. Also consider the colour of your stock and the colour of your horse's browband (if you use a coloured one), and try to match them up so they complement each other. Be careful not to go over the top; 'bling' is all about a small amount to make a statement – you don't want to blind the judge!

Making a stock.

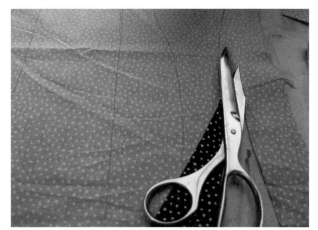

Step 1

Step 2

Step 3

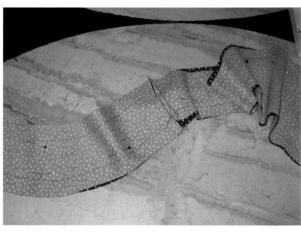

Step 4

Step 5

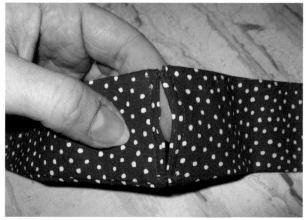

Step 6

It is possible to make your own elegant bows.

Hair accessories

Hair accessories should match the overall outfit, both in style and colour.

Show bows, nets and bungees

Long hair tucked neatly into a net and finished off with a bow can look really smart. It is possible to buy show bows and nets as one entity, and the internet is a good place to look, although again factor in the cost of postage and packaging. If you prefer to make your own however, it is easy to do and allows greater scope in choice of bow colours.

YOU WILL NEED

A plain hair slide
A length of ribbon of your choice
A hairnet
Glue
Additional decorative pieces if required

STEP 1

Plain hair slides can be bought from beading supplies shops for just a few pence, or you can salvage an old slide and remove any decorative features from the top. Choose a piece of suitable ribbon or velvet with which to make the bow. This needs to be stiff enough to hold its shape. Tie the ribbon into an even bow, and glue the centre to prevent it from coming undone. It can also be a good idea to spray with spray starch to help it keep its shape. Trim the ends of the bow, then fold the end over on itself and glue to prevent fraying.

STEP 2

The look of the bow can be further enhanced by a single motif being attached to the centre. You can buy small charms, logos or even decorative buttons relatively cheaply. Stitch or glue to the centre of the bow.

STEP 3

Plain hairnets can be purchased very cheaply. Choose one that matches as closely as possible the colour of your hair. Fold the net in two so the opening is relatively small. To attach the net to the slide, gently ease the double layer of net over the top part of the slide. Alternatively, keep the net separate from the slide, then place the net over your hair bun with the slide to secure it at the top. Some of the shop-bought nets come with diamante chips on the actual net itself, but when making your own, if you wish to jazz it up further, try giving the net a light dusting with sparkle. You will need to repeat every time you wear it. Lastly, glue the bow to the slide.

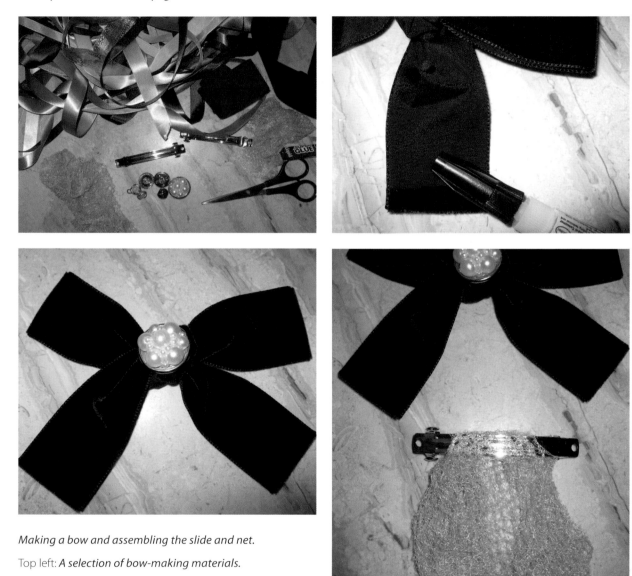

Making a bow and assembling the slide and net.

Top left: *A selection of bow-making materials.*

Top right: *Step 1*

Below left: *Step 2*

Below right: *Step 3*

An alternative hair bow

STEP 1

To make a different-shaped bow, you will need five lengths of ribbon. For the bottom layer, which attaches to the slide, measure the length alongside the size of your slide (it needs to slightly overlap each end of the slide so the slide part is hidden). Cut a fork in each end and seal either by gluing a hem or using clear nail varnish.

STEP 2

Take the next length of ribbon and cut and fold it so it is slightly shorter than the first layer. Glue the two ends of the ribbon together in the middle. Repeat this with the remaining lengths but leaving one length of ribbon to one side. Position the folded ribbons one on top of the other and staple, or stitch together in the middle.

STEP 3

Take the remaining piece of ribbon and wrap it around the middle of the other lengths and glue. Next, fix the hairnet to the slide as above, then finally glue the bow to the slide.

Clips

Clips and hair slides can be made to any design of your liking, and very cheaply. Buy the plain slides from beading supply shops, and then attach the bow of your choice as outlined in steps 1 to 3.

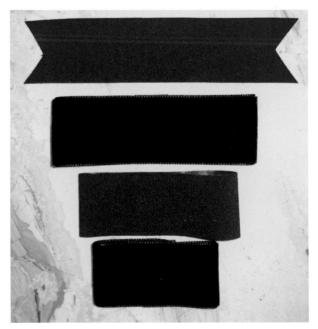

Making an alternative style of hair bow. Top left: *Step 1*

Above: *Step 2*

Left: *Step 3*

Small bows for children

For children with long hair, two pigtails can look very fetching as long as they are tightly plaited and neatly finished off. Small bows on the ends of plaits complete the picture.

YOU WILL NEED
Two lengths of ribbon
Several plain hair bands

STEP **1**
Hair bands can be bought in bulk very cheaply from virtually any supermarket or chemist. Buy bands that match the colour of the hair. Take one length of ribbon and, using a single knot, tie onto the band.

STEP **2**
Tie the ribbon into a neat bow. Then trim the ends of the ribbon, cutting a triangle or a diagonal. After trimming the ends paint them with clear nail polish to prevent fraying. Then stitch through the centre of the bow a couple of times to secure it.

The simple steps in making a bow for a child.

Bungees

Some people prefer a hairnet secured with a hair bungee, rather than a bow. Bungees are very easy to make, and can be made in the material of your choice.

YOU WILL NEED
A piece of elastic approximately ⅓ x 10½ in (1 cm x 26.5 cm)
Material of your choice, approximately 22 x 3 in (56 x 7.5 cm)
Needle and thread

STEP **1**

You can alter the dimensions of your elastic and material based on how much hair you have and how big you want the bungee to be. To work out the length of the material in relation to the length of the elastic, pull the elastic to its full stretch and measure – this will give you the length of the material needed. Take your material and hem the two short ends, then fold in half along its length and sew down the seam to join the two sides together.

STEP **2**

Turn the material the right side out and thread the elastic through the middle using a safety pin. Sew the two ends of the elastic together, stitch the join twice to strengthen it. Then carefully slide one end of the material inside the other and sew the join closed.

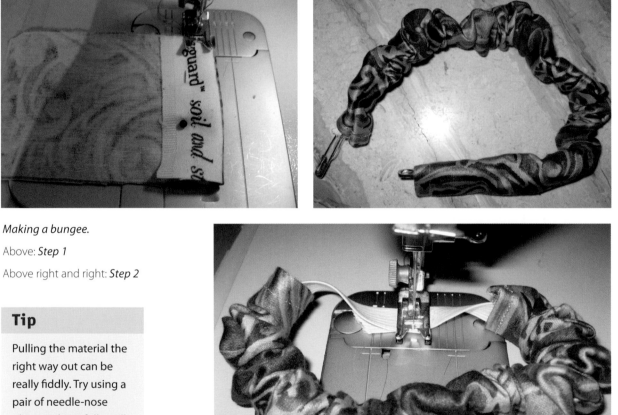

Making a bungee.

Above: *Step 1*

Above right and right: *Step 2*

Tip

Pulling the material the right way out can be really fiddly. Try using a pair of needle-nose pliers and carefully pull the material the right way, while holding the other end.

Spur straps

Those serious 'bling' addicts out there might want to consider adding a little pizzazz to your spur straps.

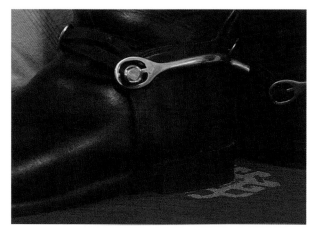

Adding a little 'bling' to the spur straps.

YOU WILL NEED

A leather hole punch

A diamante button or bead, or similar decorative feature

Beading wire or strong cotton

Needle-nose pliers

STEP **1**

The most effective place to add your decorative element is on the piece of leather that passes through the side of the spur. With the strap still in place, mark where you will need to make your hole with a leather hole punch, then remove the strap and carefully punch a small hole.

STEP **2**

Next, thread the leather back through the spur. Then place the decoration over the hole on the outside and thread your wire or cotton so it passes through the hole, the decoration and back through the hole and can be wound off against the bar of the spur. Do not over-tighten the wire as it will snap.

STEP **3**

Next re-thread the rest of the strap through the spur.

Be aware that the wire can rub the outside of your boot, so place a small square of tape or sticking plaster over the wire to protect your boot. This should be small enough so that, while it covers the wire on the inside of the spur strap, it cannot be seen.

Bear in mind that this feature is not robust and so, if possible, keep these spur straps for competing and use a different set for everyday use.

See photos overleaf ▶

Hats

Removable hat covers or silks are relatively inexpensive to buy, and with this in mind and the cost of purchasing the material and time involved it is often more economical to buy them than make them. However velvets in

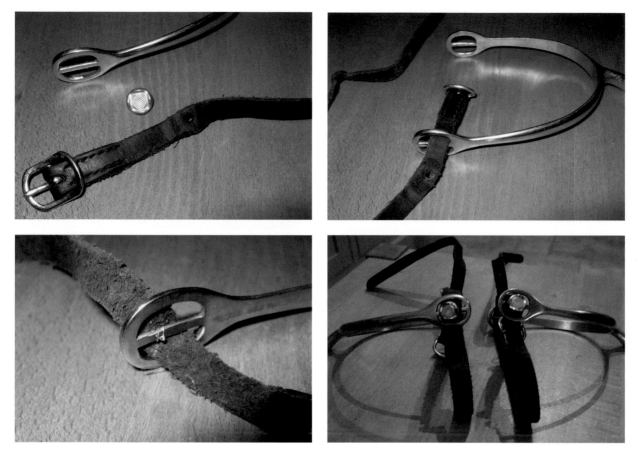

Brightening up spur straps.

Top row: *Step 1*

Below, left: *Step 2*

Below, right: *Step 3*

particular do age: they tend to become shiny, have bald spots, stain and fade. Never throw old covers out! Use old covers and add to them to create fun new silks suitable for cross-country riding. You can get really inventive and cut out spots or stars or similar logos and stitch them onto old silks to give them a whole new look.

Care of velvet hats

To keep your hat in the best condition:

- Try to store out of direct sunlight.
- Store in a cotton cover.
- Use baby wipes to remove dust and hair.
- Use shoe polish or marker pen to fill in bald spots. Alternatively, products such as suede renewal items, suede repair sprays and suede dyes work well for covering up bald bits.

Tip

Don't forget to stitch the bows up at the back of velvet hats!

- Steam over a boiling kettle then brush the pile with a soft brush to restore it to a new look.

Decorative rivets

It is worth noting, that it is possible to buy decorative rivets, which are excellent for jazzing up spur straps, browbands, headcollars and many other leather items. The initial cost of purchasing the tools required is not much provided you shop around, and is a one-off purchase, which then allows you to decorate all kinds of equipment quickly and easily. Many US companies will ship to the UK, although there are also companies in the UK such as Tandy Leather Supplies who sell suitable equipment and decorative rivets.

Care of boots

- Black rubber boots can be thoroughly scrubbed to remove grease and dirt, dried and then polished with furniture polish to give a really good shine.

- Small holes in rubber riding boots can be patched using a bicycle repair kit.

- When rubber boots perish beyond repair at the ankle, cut them down and use them as galoshes or 'muckers'.

- Try to keep leather boots in a cotton or flannel bag to keep them clean.

- Keep boot shapers in them to help them maintain their shape; alternatively roll up a magazine and stuff inside each boot.

- Every now and then, for leather boots, use a little waterproofing ointment along the seams round the foot and any other stitching.

- Keep clean with a damp cloth.

- Polish leather boots with boot polish, but not on the insides, especially if you have a grey horse.

- Treat leather occasionally with leather cream.

CHAPTER 4

Tack accessories and cleaning tips

There is always a fine balance to be struck between quality and cost, and in some areas there is simply no alternative to swallowing the cost and purchasing the best possible (in particular, feed), but there are other areas in which one can 'make do'. Furnishing the tack room, providing tack accessories and cleaning tack are areas where you can really make a difference financially.

'Never throw anything away' is a maxim that bears fruit in many areas of yard management and the tack room is no exception. For example, tack rooms can be fitted out cheaply using cast-off kitchen cabinets. Often, during house renovations, cabinets are ripped out and thrown away, but they can actually serve really well in the tack room. Try approaching builders or property developers to see if they will let you salvage units that can then be installed in the tack or feed room area. The tack room is a place where a fair amount of time is spent, so it pays to try to make it as clean, comfortable and pleasant as possible to work in. Sometimes simply repainting an interior with white or light-coloured paint can give it a whole new, more modern look. Paint, too, can be expensive, so look for bin ends on offer, and remember to wash the cans out after use and keep them…just in case!

Bridle accessories

Bridle pegs

Bridle pegs are really easy to make and can be fashioned in a number of different ways. The main consideration is that they provide a smooth and curved surface for the bridle to rest on so that the shape of the headpiece is not compromised.

Pattern one

YOU WILL NEED

Old, empty and washed out tins of saddle soap, with their lids, or similar sized tins
Washers
Drill, small drill bit and screws or nails
Piece of wood
Marker pen

STEP 1

The old-fashioned saddle soap tins make excellent bridle pegs and are attractive and unusual to look at in the tack room. The pegs will need to be fixed to wood, so you will need to screw a piece of suitable sized wood of the desired length to the wall. Mark along the length of wood where the pegs will sit and remember to leave enough room in between them.

STEP 2

You can either fix the tins with a nail or screws. I prefer to use screws. Hold the tin in place on the wood, and make two small holes in the back of it using the drill bit, or if you are careful you can screw the screws straight in. Then place a washer over each hole and screw in the screws. Alternatively, drive two nails in.

STEP 3

Put the lid back on the tin with the logo on display.

Empty tins fixed to the wall make excellent bridle pegs.

The finished peg.

Pattern two

YOU WILL NEED

The cast-off pieces from a rounded fence post
Several metal plates
Sandpaper
Screws
Drill, drill bit
Marker pen
A 2 x 4 in (5 x 10 cm) plank

STEP 1

Check to see if local timber companies have any cast off pieces cut from rounded fence posts; often they will just give them away. These make ideal bridle pegs. Cut them into sections approximately 2–2½ in (5–6.3 cm) wide. Sand the edges if necessary to smooth them off.

STEP 2

Mark on the 2 x 4 in (5 x 10 cm) plank the intervals where the pegs need to sit. On the back of the pieces of wood on each side screw the metal plate. You might find it easier to pre-drill the holes.

STEP 3

Attach the wooden pieces to the 2 x 4 in (5 x 10 cm) plank by screwing the plate to the wood.

> **Tip**
>
> When hanging bridles, use dark-coloured elastic bands underneath bridle keepers to stop them slipping down.

Bridle covers

Keeping bridles (and saddles) neatly stored and covered helps to keep them clean, in good condition and prevents the leather from fading. Bridle and saddle covers are particularly useful when travelling to shows, etc., to keep them neat and free from dust. One of the easiest ways to cover bridles is to simply use an old pillow, put the bridle inside and pull together the ends of the pillowcase with an elastic band.

Pattern one

YOU WILL NEED

A piece of material 34 x 12 in (86 cm x 30 cm)
A piece of material 34 x 6½ in (86 x 16.5 cm)

A piece of material 34 x 6½ in (86 x 16.5 cm)
A zip approximately 22 in (56 cm)
A double-ended ('S') hook, an old sock, old nylons or stuffing
Needle, thread and sharp scissors

STEP **1**

Cut out your pieces of material. Piece A is the large back piece, and pieces B and C the front pieces. The extra ½ in (1.25 cm) is to allow for hems and the zip.

STEP **2**

Inserting a hook is optional. It can be useful for transporting bridles to shows, etc, but the bridle should not be stored for long periods on a hook like this as it is not the right shape for the headpiece. Buy a two-ended hook. These are usually available very cheaply from hardware shops. Take an old nylon and thread over the hook, then stuff with stuffing to pad the hook out and pull an old sock over it, securing with an elastic band.

STEP **3**

Take pieces B and C and stitch together along the vertical inside seam. Stitch roughly 6 in (15 cm) from the top and bottom, and then sew the zip into the remaining hole.

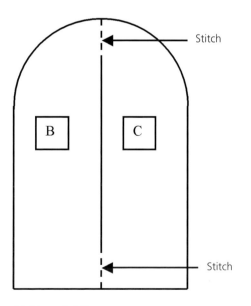

Making a bridle cover.

STEP 4

Place piece B/C over piece A with the right sides facing in and stitch all around the perimeter leaving a small hole at the top, through which you will insert the hook.

STEP 5

Turn the material the right way out, insert the hook and hang up your bridle.

Pattern two

YOU WILL NEED

A piece of material 34 x 12 in (86 cm x 30 cm)
A piece of material 34 x 7½ in (86 cm x 19 cm)
A piece of material 34 x 6½ in (86 x 16.5 cm)
A double-ended ('S') hook, an old sock, old nylons or stuffing
Needle, thread and sharp scissors

STEP 1

Cut out your pieces of material. You don't have to round the top end; you can leave it square if you prefer. Piece A is the large back piece, piece B is the wider of the front pieces and piece C the smallest piece.

STEP 2

Take the 'S' hook and cover the bottom half with padding held in place with a nylon. For extra padding, place an old sock over this and secure in place with an elastic band.

STEP 3

Hem down what will form the inside of the long side of piece B and C and around their curved ends. Next, hem the curved end of large piece A. Place piece B and C together so that their inside edges overlap and stitch down approximately 6 in (15 cm) from the top and bottom.

STEP 4

Place the three pieces one on top of the other with their inner sides facing outwards. Stitch around the outside edge leaving a small gap just large enough to thread the 'S' hook through. Then turn the bag the right way round, insert the 'S' hook and hang up your bridle.

See photos opposite ▶

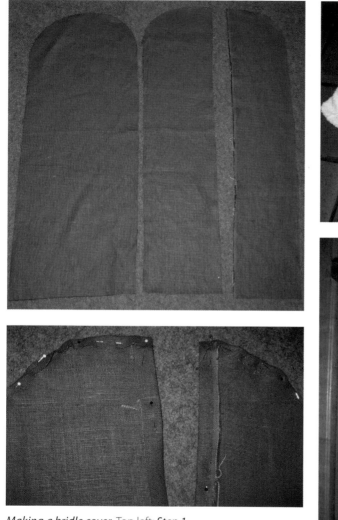

Making a bridle cover. Top left: *Step 1*

Top right: *Step 2*

Below left: *Step 3*

Right: *Step 4*

Saddle accessories

Saddle racks

These are slightly more complicated to make than bridle pegs, but are still not too daunting. The thing to weigh up is the cost/time involved, as currently saddle racks can be bought for just a few pounds or dollars. With this in mind, when attempting to cut costs it is important to try to garner the materials needed for next to nothing, and this can involve a trip to the local timber yard and a rifle through their off-cuts. Again, often they will give discarded pieces of wood away, or charge just a nominal amount.

How to make a saddle rack

YOU WILL NEED

A piece of wood 2 x 4 x 30 in (5 x 10 x 76 cm) for the back plate (piece A)
A piece of wood 2 x 2 x 18 in (5 x 5 x 45 cm) for the saddle rest (piece B)
A piece of wood 2 x 2 x 24 in (5 x 5 x 61 cm) for the saddle rest support (piece C)
Five metal corner brackets
Drill and drill bit
Saw
Some 4 in (10 cm) screws and 2 in (5 cm) screws
One piece of thick foam 6 x 18 in (15 cm x 45 cm) and a piece of synthetic
    sheepskin approximately 10 x 20 in (26 cm x 50 cm)
A vice is not essential, but makes things easier

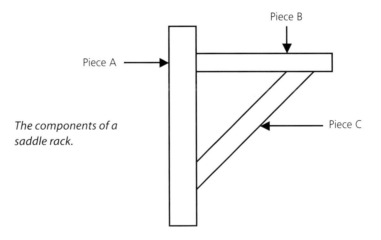

The components of a saddle rack.

STEP 1
Measure and cut out piece A, the back board and piece B, the saddle rest.

STEP 2
Measure 6½ in (16.5 cm) from one end of the 2 x 4 in (5 x 10 cm) wood and draw a light pencil line on both sides of piece A. Next, measure 1 in (2.5 cm) in from each side and make another mark on both sides of piece A. Sit piece B on the marked area and draw around the perimeter on both sides of piece A. You now have a square on the front and back of piece A. Make two crosses on what will be the back of piece A.

STEP **3**

Take a suitable sized drill bit and drill where your two crosses are through piece A. Next take your two 4 in (10 cm) screws and screw them in until their points are just poking through the other side of piece A.

STEP **4**

Take piece B and, holding it over the marked area, push down firmly onto the two screw ends. When you remove the piece you should have two indentations where the screws need to go. Now drill your holes to approximately 1 in (2.5 cm) into the end of piece B.

STEP **5**

Place piece B in a vice and piece A over the top so that the screws in piece A fit into the tops of the holes in piece B. Now screw the screws in tightly.

STEP **6**

Screw one bracket on the top of piece B to further attach it to piece A.

STEP **7**

Lay piece A/B on its side and place piece C diagonally to meet both A and B (see diagram). Draw a line at the top and bottom of the piece to indicate the angle at which the wood needs to be cut, then carefully saw along the line. Sand the cut edge flat so it fits snugly in between piece A/B.

STEP **8**

Screw piece C onto piece A/B. Now take the piece of foam and place over piece B, securing with glue, roofing tacks or a staple gun. Finally, cover the foam with the synthetic sheepskin and then fix the saddle rack to the wall using the remaining four corner brackets. *See photos overleaf* ▶

Making a saddle rack.

Step 2

Step 4

Far left: *Step 5*

Left: *Step 6*

Step 7

Step 7 continued

Step 8

The finished rack.

Saddle covers

As with bridles, it really pays to keep saddles covered. To avoid problems with mould, use natural fabrics, not plastic. The easiest way to cover a saddle is to simply cut down an old bed sheet and drape it or wrap it, or alternatively make a cover to measure.

How to make a saddle cover

YOU WILL NEED

A piece of material 6 ft 6 in x 36 in wide (2 m x 91 cm)

A 36 in (91 cm) zip

Paper and marker pen to make a pattern

Scissors

Needle and thread (sewing machine is preferable!)

STEP 1

Mark out your saddle-shaped pattern on the paper (see diagram) and cut out. Fold the material in half and place the pattern on top. Draw around the pattern twice so you have two saddle shapes on the folded material. Then cut out the material. You should now have two *pairs* of saddle shapes. NB: this pattern is geared towards a 17–18 in (43–45 cm) saddle; for a 16 in (40.5 cm) saddle take off ½ in (1.25 cm) all the way around, and for a 15 in (38 cm) saddle take off 1 in (2.5 cm) all the way round. *See photos overleaf* ▶

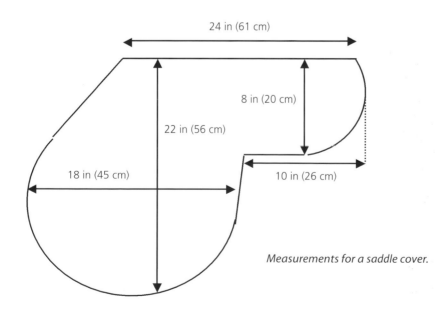

24 in (61 cm)

8 in (20 cm)

22 in (56 cm)

18 in (45 cm)

10 in (26 cm)

Measurements for a saddle cover.

STEP 2

Keep the material with the right sides facing inwards and stitch along the top line (effectively from pommel to cantle) on each pair.

STEP 3

Next, if you wish to make handles, do so now. Cut out two 12 x 4 in (30 x 10 cm) pieces of the material. Fold each piece in half along its length and, with the right side of the material facing outwards, turn a small hem inwards along the lengths and stitch together. It can help to iron the hems flat before stitching. If you wish to bolster the handles, thread a piece of soft cotton rope through each.

STEP 4

Spread the two saddle patterns out on top of each other with the right side facing inwards, and the handles on the inside, as shown in the photos. Stitch the two pieces together leaving a stretch along the pommel end of the material into which the zip will be sewn. Now iron down a hem along the open zip section and turn the cover the right way out.

STEP 5

Pin the zip into place and stitch down.

If you chose to put handles on the cover, and will be carrying it as if a bag, then make sure that you choose fabric that is of a sufficient weight to cope with this. If it is just to function as a cover then it is not necessary to add handles, and the material may be of a lighter weight.

Making a saddle cover.

Step 1

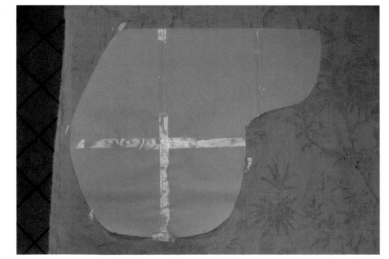

Step 2

Step 4

Step 4 continued

Step 5

Step 5 continued

The finished saddle cover.

Storing leather items and rugs

Leather

One of the biggest problems when storing leather items of tack that are not in frequent use is moulding. The best way to avoid mould and mildew forming on tack is to make sure the tack room is dry and well ventilated. If it is not possible or economical to keep the tack room at a sufficient temperature then it is worthwhile transferring little-used leather items into a corner of the house. It is not just the winter, however, that causes problems: a hot and humid summer is just as likely to lead to mould problems unless a dehumidifier is used, but this is not always a practical or economical solution. As mentioned earlier, keeping leather tack clean and covered in cotton is helpful in combating mould and also preventing dust problems.

Before storing leather items clean them thoroughly and dress the leather with a good leather conditioner. Leather conditioner is preferable to leather oils, unless the leather is seriously dried out and cracked. Once they have been put away, try to get into a routine of checking them every month or so to make sure no mould has formed and wipe them down with a glycerine saddle soap.

Rugs and blankets

Although leather items should never be stored in plastic containers, large plastic containers can be useful for storing rugs and blankets, but make sure that anything that goes into them is completely dry before being stored. However, for preference, try using old travelling trunks instead. These can often be picked up at auctions or second-hand shops very cheaply, and they make good storage facilities.

When storing anything in trunks or plastic containers also insert a small bag of silica gel, which will absorb moisture, and mothballs. Always make sure that rugs are cleaned before being put away for the winter or the summer, and make any repairs or alterations necessary before storing them so next time they are needed they are in good working order.

Making blanket racks

Single blanket racks can be really useful when attached to the outside of the stable or stall and are relatively easy to make.

Pattern one

YOU WILL NEED

Two pieces of wood to form the ends: any scraps will do provided they are robust
    enough – I have used pieces 2 x 4 x 5 in (5 x 10 x 12.5 cm)
A piece of 1 x 36 in (2.5 cm x 91 cm) dowel or a broom handle
A drill and flat wood drill bit
Eight metal corner braces, 1 in (2.5 cm) size
Saw
Sanding paper or sander

STEP 1

Try sorting through a local timber yards off-cuts to see if you can find two
suitable pieces of wood. Smooth the ends with a sander, then mark the
position of the hole needed to insert the dowel. This needs to be about 2.5 in
(6.3 cm) in from the edge.

STEP 2

Sand the wood smooth so there are no splinters or rough edges. Take the flat
wood bit and measure 1 in (2.5 cm) from the cutting end and mark with a
piece of electrical tape. This is the guide to how deep the hole needs to be
drilled. Then take the drill and with the flat wood bit in place drill an inden-
tation into each piece of wood to a depth of 1 in (2.5 cm).

STEP 3

Screw your fixing plates to the back edge of the two pieces of wood. Attach
the first piece of wood to the outside of the stable, or where it is needed, at
the desired height, and out of reach of the horse. Insert the dowel/broom
handle and then place the second piece of wood on other end. Make sure the
fit is tight so the dowel cannot slip out, then screw the second wooden piece
to the wall. *See photos overleaf* ▶

Pattern two: alternative blanket/brushing boot/ numnah rack

YOU WILL NEED

Two, thee or four pieces of 1 x 36 in (2.5 x 91 cm) dowel or old broom handles
Drill and drill bit
Vice
11½ ft (3.5 m) of ¼ in (6 mm) rope (preferably nylon)

Making a blanket rack, pattern one.

Step 1

Step 2

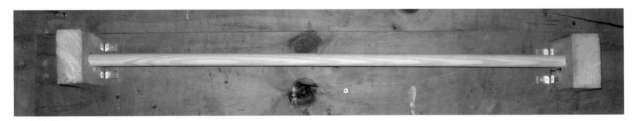

Left and above: *Step 3*

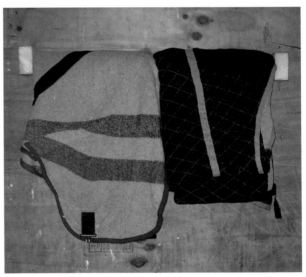

The finished blanket rack.

STEP 1

This is a portable rug rack that can be hung up in the tack room or on the outside of a stable and is useful for rugs, numnahs and bandages. You can essentially make it with as few or many horizontal pieces as you like, but three tends to work well. Clamp your dowel in a vice if possible, then drill a hole 2 in (5 cm) in from the end of each piece of wood. Sand the back of the holes if necessary.

STEP 2

Lay your dowels in a line on the floor with roughly 14 in (35.5 cm) space between each piece.

Take the rope and fold it in half, then tie a knot in the end leaving a small loop – this is the top of the rope and will be used for hanging the rack on a firmly fastened screw-fitting hook. Position the knot in the middle of your first piece of dowel, then thread through the top piece and tie a knot underneath at each end. Make sure the rope is even on both sides. It can be easier to hang the rack at this stage. Then, approximately 13 in (33 cm) further down, thread the rope through the next piece of dowel and secure with a knot. Do the same for the last piece of dowel.

STEP 3

Trim the ends of the rope and, if necessary and the rope used is nylon, pass through a flame to stop them from fraying. *See photos overleaf* ▶

Making a blanket rack, pattern two.

Step 1

Step 2

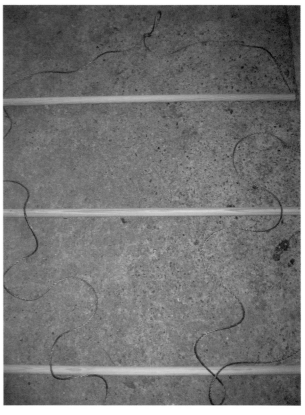

Step 2 continued

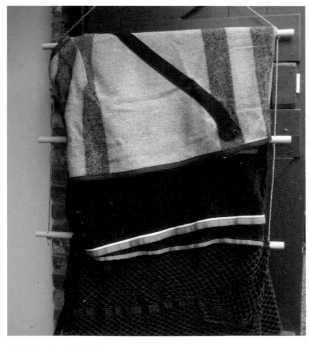

The finished blanket rack

Step 3

Tips for cleaning tack

Provided tack gets 'proper' and correct attention on a regular basis (that is, full cleaning using a glycerine soap and nourishing with a leather cream), you can get away with some less accepted methods in between.

- Very dirty tack can be washed in a mixture of water with washing-up liquid and a little oil, before being towel-dried and cleaned with saddle soap.

- Washing-up liquid in your water will help cut grease.

- For stubborn jockeys (accumulations of grease) apply washing-up liquid neat to the spot, or remove using a fingernail or the back of a knife.

- In general, try not to get leather too wet as it causes it to stretch, and it can crack if it dries out too rapidly. If you do get it very wet then towel it dry immediately.

- Damage is done to leather when it dries out too quickly (if set next to a radiator for example).

- Glycerine saddle soap is amongst the best to use: apply it with a damp (not wet) sponge and work into the leather.

- Clean buckles with metal polish, and buff them.

- Check all stitching, buckles, buckle holes and webbing when cleaning tack.

- Apply a leather cream after cleaning tack with soap, but wait for the tack to dry before applying.

- Neatsfoot oil is excellent for very dry or cracked leather, but don't overuse as it can cause the leather to stretch and become 'soggy'.

- Clean tooling on Western tack with a soft toothbrush.

- After cleaning Western saddles, twist the stirrup fenders out and secure by running an old broom handle through them.

- The saddle horn on Western saddles can be prone to knocks and bangs, so when storing or transporting the saddle place an old sock over the saddle horn. You can even push some stuffing into the end of the sock to provide further protection.

- Western saddles (in particular new ones) can have a tendency to squeak, which is irritating. To combat this, turn the saddle upside down on a clean, soft surface, move the stirrup fenders to one side and shake some talcum powder in the area between the fenders and the jockeys, and a little to the skirts.

- Take tack completely apart at least once a month to clean thoroughly.

- Stirrups can rub against the saddle flaps when run up; to prevent this take an old sock and pull over each stirrup. This will also help to keep them shiny.

- After exercise, don't throw sweaty numnahs over the saddle to dry off – it is not good for the leather.

- Keep natural sheepskin numnahs clean by sprinkling with baby powder.

- Some household soap-cleaning products can be used to clean leather. A US example is Murphy's oil: it cleans well, is economical and removes grease, but used long-term it will dry the leather out, so it must be used in conjunction with a nourishing cream.

- Toothpaste can be used to polish up metal pieces on tack including the bit rings, metal saddle studs, stirrup bars, stirrups and buckles. Use a toothbrush to scrub the area then rinse carefully with a cloth, and polish.

- After cleaning tack for a show, spray on hairspray (not to the seat of the saddle). This will keep the tack shiny and prevent a build-up of dirt.

Full tack cleaning procedure

Take tack apart.

Clean first with water and a little washing-up detergent and a clean cloth.

Towel dry.

Soap with glycerine and a slightly damp cloth (make sure it's not too wet).

Every few weeks follow this with a nourishing leather cream – less is more, don't overdo the quantity of cream.

Clean buckles, bits and stirrups and towel dry.

Re-assemble tack, having first checked all stitching, buckles, buckle holes and webbing.

Store in warm, dry room, preferably covered.

Cleaning economies

Making saddle soap go further

Take a bar of glycerine saddle soap and place in a saucepan with ½ pint (0.28 litre) of milk. Heat over a medium temperature until the soap melts and the two can be blended together, then carefully pour into a suitable container. The mixture will cool and set creating a creamy saddle soap that can be applied using a cloth as normal (or even just your fingers).

Make your own saddle soap

Formula one

YOU WILL NEED

2 pints (1.14 litres) water
24 tbsp (360 ml) soap flakes (available very cheaply from supermarkets)
8 fl oz (228 ml) melted beeswax
4 fl oz (114 ml) neatsfoot oil

STEP 1

Combine the neatsfoot oil and beeswax in a double boiler (or heat over a very low heat) to melt the beeswax and stir thoroughly.

STEP 2

Bring the water to a fast boil, then reduce to a simmer and add the soap flakes gradually, stirring vigorously.

STEP 3

Remove from heat and add the melted beeswax and neatsfoot mixture to the soap solution. Stir thoroughly then pour into suitable containers such as old shoe polish (or saddle soap) tins and allow to cool.

Formula two

YOU WILL NEED

6¼ tbsp (94 ml) beeswax
10 tbsp (150 ml) sodium hydroxide (US flake lye)
20 tbsp (300 ml) water
2 tbsp (30 ml) soap flakes
15 tbsp (225 ml) turpentine

Tip

Not a cleaning tip, but one to make life easier. When using pull-on overreach boots, spray the insides of them with cooking oil to make them easier to pull on and off, and smear a little Vaseline around the top to stop them chaffing.

STEP 1

Combine the beeswax, half of the water (10 tbsp/150 ml) and the sodium hydroxide in a pan and boil for 5 minutes, stirring constantly.

STEP 2

Boil the remaining water in a separate pan and add the soap flakes. Once they are thoroughly mixed gradually add them to the sodium hydroxide and beeswax solution, mixing thoroughly.

STEP 3

Remove from the heat and stir in the turpentine, then pour the mixture into suitable containers or jars.

Uses for baking soda and vinegar

These two household items are really useful around the stable yard and are extremely economical and non-toxic.

Baking soda

Baking soda is a really good cleaning agent.

- Use it to remove stable stains (see Chapter 1).

- Make a thick baking soda paste by adding a small quantity of water and treat manure/sweat/mud stains on rugs or numnahs. Smear over the offending area and leave to dry before washing as normal.

- Use it to clean feed and water buckets; it will remove dirt without leaving any trace of smell or taste.

- Sprinkle a small amount of it in the bottom of your waste bins in the tack/feed room as it will absorb odours.

- Use it to clean bits and stirrups.

- Sprinkle a small amount onto a damp cloth for cleaning surfaces in the tack/feed room, then rinse with plain water.

- Use half your normal quantity of laundry soap and top-up the other half with baking soda to cut though stains and grease.

- Pour ¼ cup of baking soda down your drains every week, followed by a bucket of hot water to help keep them clear.

Vinegar

Vinegar is also incredibly versatile and can be used in a number of ways around the stable yard.

- As discussed in Chapter 1, vinegar can be added to a homemade shampoo mix, or to rinse water.

- Apple cider vinegar added to the feed promotes good health and acts as an anti-oxidant.

- Use a dilution of half white vinegar and half water mixed in a spray bottle to clean stable, tack room and feed room windows and various surfaces. Spray on and wipe off with newspaper or an old piece of cotton.

- Use to clean dirty bits as outlined under Cleaning Bits, next section.

- Use vinegar to repel flies, see Chapter 5.

- An old-fashioned treatment is one cupful of vinegar in the horse's drinking water which is said to repel flies and have a generally good effect on health. (Some people give cider vinegar to horses with low-level arthritic conditions, apparently with good effect.) However, you must make sure the horse gets used to the flavour and is not put off from drinking.

- Add ½ cup of vinegar to your laundry soap to help combat stubborn stains, keep colours bright and prevent 'balling' of soft fabrics.

- Pour a cup of vinegar down your drains weekly; allow to sit for 30 minutes then flush with cold water to remove odours.

Cleaning bits

- Clean bits using a mixture of 3 parts baking soda to 1 part water. Apply the paste using a soft toothbrush and scrub, then rinse with warm water and polish with a soft cloth. The same process can be used on stirrups.

- For seriously dirty bits and to remove scale, use the following mix. Dissolve one tsp (5 ml) of salt in one cup of vinegar and then add plain flour to create a paste. Cover the bit with the paste and let it sit for 10 minutes, then scrub with an old toothbrush, rinse with warm water and polish with a soft cloth.

- Alternatively for scaly bits use tomato ketchup. Squirt a little ketchup in a small dish, take an old toothbrush, dip in the ketchup and then scrub the bit. For really stubborn dirt coat the area in ketchup and leave for 15 minutes, then rinse with warm water and polish with a soft cloth.

- Metal bits can also be cleaned by running them through the dishwasher, but be sure to rinse them thoroughly and polish with a soft cloth after they have been through a cycle.

- Alternatively, boil a pan of water on the stove, place the bit in the boiling water and simmer for 5 minutes to remove dirt. Drain, rinse under cold water and then using a toothbrush (or an old nail brush) scrub any remaining residue away, rinse and polish.

- An old-fashioned method of cleaning bits is to bury them in a bucket with 2–3 cups of whole oats, then scrub the oats against the bit to remove dried-on grass and saliva residue.

CHAPTER 5

Health and first aid

The horse's health and well-being is the first and foremost priority, and a veterinary surgeon should be consulted in any situation if there is cause for concern that is beyond sensible stable management and first aid practices. The recipes in this chapter for homemade ointments, and tips on aspects of first aid, including tricks for administering oral medication, should be used in conjunction with veterinary advice where necessary. Although many superficial cuts, bumps and bruises can be treated by the responsible horse owner, always use common sense.

The horse's health is the first priority.

Equine vital statistics

Temperature 100–101°F (approx 38°C)

Pulse (resting) 32–42 beats per minute (adult horse)

Respiration (resting) 8–14 breaths per minute

These are approximate and will vary slightly from horse to horse.

When to call the vet

Call the vet if:

- There is any deviation from the horse's normal vital statistics (see above).
- The horse is bleeding profusely, or has an injury that is anything other than minor.

- The horse is exhibiting signs of colic.

- The horse is dehydrated.

- The horse has poor capillary refill (which may be indicative of various disorders as well as dehydration).

- The horse is not drinking and/or eating.

- The horse has rapid weight loss or weight gain.

- The horse has thick discharge coming down its nose.

- The horse is coughing excessively.

- The horse has an eye injury and/or excessive discharge from the eye, and/or the eyes are sunken or dull.

- The horse is reluctant to move.

- The horse is behaving erratically including wobbling, circling, weakness in the hindquarters or other unusual behaviour.

- The horse is significantly lame.

Hot and cold treatments

Poultices

Poultices are most commonly used on the lower limbs or the feet and can be applied to open wounds, or to strain and sprain injuries. There are a number of different types of poultice, some of which can be made at home. They can be used hot, in which case they aid healing through increasing blood supply to the injury site, act as a drawing agent and relieve pain, or can be used cold to reduce inflammation and pain. One of the most widely used commercial poultices is Animalintex, which works best as a hot poultice or as a dry wound dressing.

How to make a bran poultice

As with most homemade recipes, this is an old-fashioned poultice that works very well. The only downside to it is that bran is edible and enjoyed by horses, so it can be advisable to apply an anti-chewing spray (see Anti-chew Treatments, later this chapter) to the outside of the bandages to discourage the horse from helping itself. Bran poultices are most often used on the feet to draw out an abscess.

YOU WILL NEED

A clean bucket

Bran

Epsom salts

Boiling water

Either a strong plastic bag or the corner of a nylon feed bag, or a
  plastic-covered nappy

Packing tape

Gamgee

Bandage material

STEP **1**

Fill a clean bucket to approximately one quarter full with two parts wheat
bran to one part Epsom salts.

STEP **2**

Pour enough boiling water into the bran to create a soft and crumbly mix.
Do not make it too wet.

STEP **3**

Empty the mixture into either the corner of an old nylon feed sack, or into a
disposable nappy. Once the mixture has cooled sufficiently (it should still be
hot, but not hot enough to burn), insert the horse's foot into the bag/nappy
and secure the top around the fetlock using packing tape. Wrapping the foot
in an old plastic bag will help to keep the heat in. Cover the foot and up over
the fetlock with Gamgee and apply a self-adhesive bandage. Bolster the toe
of the foot with packing tape.

Tip

Disposable nappies
make excellent band-
ages for the feet, as do
recycled old nylon feed
sacks, or – even better –
the hessian ones. The
hoof is placed in the
nappy and the nappy is
then secured around
the pastern. Further
bandaging or duct tape
is used over the top of
the nappy to secure it
and keep the dressing
clean.

*Disposable nappies make
excellent dressings or
bandages for the feet.*

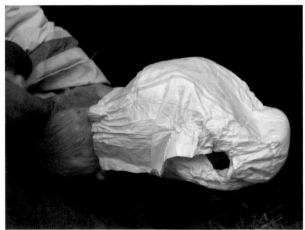

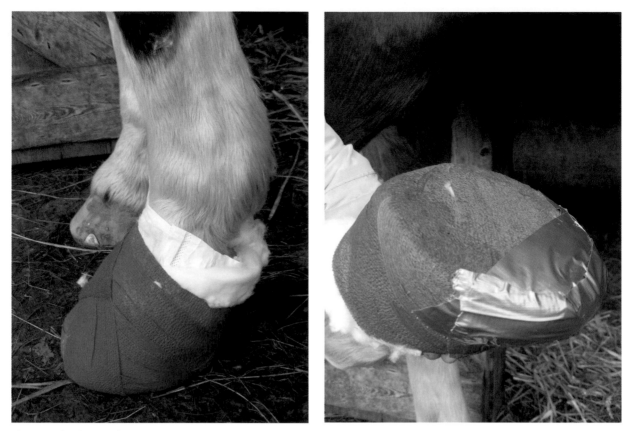

Above and right: *Bandaging a foot with a poultice in place.*

Poultices should be changed twice daily, and a horse with a poultice on should be kept stabled.

How to make a potato poultice

YOU WILL NEED

Two unpeeled potatoes
Two pieces of old cotton material, cheesecloth or thick gauze
An old plastic bag
Gamgee
Bandage material

STEP 1

Cut the potatoes into cubes and boil. Remove from heat and mash.

STEP 2

Spread the mashed potato between the two pieces of material to form a pad.

Ingredients for a potato poultice.

STEP **3**

Allow the pad to cool sufficiently to be applied safely, then apply to either the foot or leg injury, as relevant. Cover the area with the plastic bag, then apply the Gamgee and bandage over the top. If using on the foot, bolster the toe of the bandage with packing tape.

Other poultice recipes

Poultice paste

The following can be used to make a poultice paste, which is then sandwiched between two pieces of cotton material and applied to the injury site.

1. Mix Epsom Salts with enough hot water to form a paste.

2. Mix sodium bicarbonate (baking soda) with enough witch hazel to form a paste.

Sugardine

Sugardine is a really effective poultice that, in particular, promotes healing, encourages the growth of healthy tissue, is excellent for use on burns, and has anti-bacterial properties; it is also useful for treating thrush. Mix a small amount of Betadine (or povidone-iodine product) with white granulated sugar to form a paste and apply to the injured area. Around 1 part Betadine to 2 parts sugar produces a decent, paste-like consistency.

Honey

Honey is also a useful natural dressing for wounds, which again has anti-bacterial properties and can help to heal wounds quickly with a minimal amount of scar tissue. Manuka honey and honey that has not been over-pasteurised is the best, and can be applied directly to the site of injury. Keep the wound covered to prevent nuisance from flies.

Leg sweats

Leg sweats can be used in place of a hot poultice, and work by creating heat, which promotes healing by increasing the blood supply to the area. The pressure of the bandage also helps in reducing inflammation and provides support to the limb. Leg sweats should *not* be used on an open injury, and should only be used on the directive of a veterinary surgeon. There are a number of different substances that can be used in the leg sweat preparation, and the veterinary surgeon will advise on the best ones. Below is a general recipe.

YOU WILL NEED

A preparation of DMSO (dimethyl sulphoxide) and nitrofurazone
Clingfilm (US Saran wrap)
Gamgee
Bandage material

STEP 1

Make sure the leg is thoroughly clean, then apply the sweat preparation.

STEP 2

Cover the whole area with a wrap or two of clean Clingfilm. The sweat preparation may have a transferring effect i.e., it has the ability to transfer minuscule particles of dirt through the skin (in very unscientific terms!) so the whole area must be extremely clean, and this is why Clingfilm or even a sterile dressing should be used to cover it instead of the usual recycled and possibly contaminated plastic bag.

STEP 3

Apply a layer of Gamgee over the Clingfilm and then bandage with self-adhesive wrap material over the top. The bandage should be left on for about 12 hours (no longer than this), although this should be at the directive of the veterinary surgeon.

Note:

- *Always wear gloves when handling DMSO.*
- *Some horses will react to DMSO, in which case remove the bandage, thoroughly wash the leg and seek veterinary advice.*

Cold packs

Cold packs and cold therapy generally are important parts of the treatment for sprains, strains, bruises and other soft tissue traumas. This form of therapy has been around for a long time, first being described by the Greek physician Hippocrates in the fourth century BC. It works by reducing inflammation, decreasing tissue damage and temporarily alleviating pain. There are a number of different cold packs on the market, most of which are expensive but they are reusable and generally work well. It is possible to make your own cold packs.

Kaolin cold packs

Kaolin (a soft white clay) poultice material is relatively expensive, but is an excellent hot or cold poultice, and can be re-used many times as a cold pack. Thus the initial expenditure is worth it in the long run. However, before buying a tub do a quick price-check; sometimes splitting a tub between two people is an option.

YOU WILL NEED

Kaolin poultice
Two pieces of cotton
Recycled plastic bag
Gamgee
Bandage material

STEP 1

Smear a thick layer of kaolin paste in a rectangular shape approximately 4 x 6 in (10 x 15 cm) between the two pieces of material and freeze.

STEP 2

When the cold pack is required, remove from the freezer and mould to the back of the horse's leg. Wrap in a recycled plastic bag.

> **Tip**
>
> Kaolin can be used as a hot poultice too. Place the tub of kaolin in a pan of hot water and heat through. Smear a thick layer between two pieces of cotton and allow it to cool enough to be applied over the injury. Hold in place with a plastic bag, Gamgee and a bandage.

STEP 3

Apply Gamgee over the top and bandage the leg. The cold pack will stay usefully cold for approximately 15 minutes. Keep at least four packs in the freezer ready-made for emergencies. As the first pack loses its coolness, remove and replace with a fresh pack.

Ice bandages

This is an effective way of applying cold therapy to the leg and can be used to replace hosing.

YOU WILL NEED

A cotton tea towel (or a Tubigrip)
Gauze bandage material and a piece of electrical tape
Packing tape
An inner tube cut to the approximate length of the leg from below the knee to
    the pastern*

* This will need to be large enough to fit the foot through so, unless you are treating a very small pony (in which case a motorcycle tyre might suit), a car inner tube works best. Although some modern car tyres don't have inner tubes, many small, local garages have a pile of them and are happy to give them away.

STEP 1

Wrap the tea towel around the leg (you can alternatively use a Tubigrip) and hold in place with a light wrap of gauze and a piece of electrical tape.

STEP 2

Roll the inner tube over the horse's foot and up its leg with the tube's outer curve to the back of the leg.

STEP 3

Fold the inner tube over the pastern and secure with packing tape. Fill the inner tube with ice cubes and then secure the top of the tube with a bandage.

The ice will gradually melt, providing cold therapy for approximately 20 minutes. Make sure the horse is standing in a wash stall or a stall without bedding, or on a well-draining piece of land. Take great care when securing the inner tube with the bandage that it is not too tight, as some shrinkage may occur when it becomes wet.

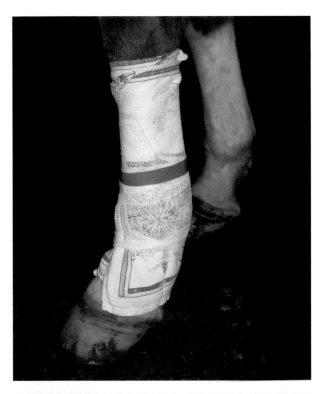

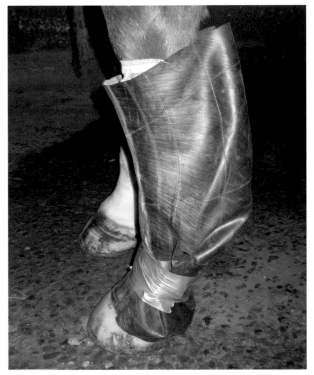

Making an ice bandage.

Above left: *Step 1*

Above right: *Step 2*

Left: *Step 3*

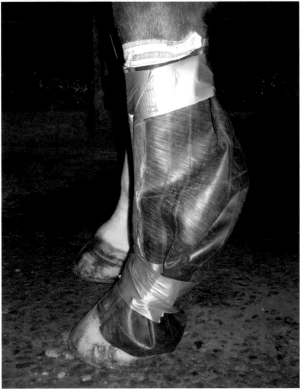

Warning

Never administer bute to a horse before the vet has seen it as it will mask the extent of lameness.

Feet and lameness

The feet are a major area of equine lameness, and good hoof care is essential to the overall soundness and health of the horse. In any case of lameness (where the cause is not immediately obvious) check the feet first. Thoroughly pick the feet out, and while doing so check for any heat that might indicate an infection. The feet should be scrubbed clean with plain water, or a weak Hibiscrub solution. Check to make sure there are no foreign bodies, such as a nail, embedded in the feet. In any event, where a foreign body is discovered, the horse must be seen by a vet. There is a huge risk of infection with foreign bodies, and also a risk that they might have punctured the internal structures of the foot. The horse will thus require an anti-tetanus shot.

If possible, and provided the horse will not be injured further (e.g. by a heavily protruding foreign object), the object should be left in place until the vet arrives. This will allow the vet to see exactly where the puncture is and how deep it is, which will assist in making an accurate assessment of the damage. If the object is likely to cause further injury by being left in, then remove it carefully, but note the angle at which it penetrated the foot, and its exact location. In most instances the vet will advise a routine of soaking the foot, generally in an Epsom salt solution, and poulticing, both of which serve to draw out any infection.

Soaking

Making soak solution

Epsom salts is one of the best soak solutions to use owing to its drawing qualities. However, for an Epsom salt solution to work efficiently it must be a saturated solution.

YOU WILL NEED

A clean bucket
Warm water
Epsom salts
A wooden spoon

STEP **1**

Fill the bucket with sufficient water to cover the injury, but no more than is necessary. It is best to use warm water, making sure the temperature is not too hot by testing it with the back of your hand.

Tetanus

Tetanus toxoid vaccinations should be given every 2 years, once the horse has completed its initial vaccination course. (In the US, tetanus toxoid is usually given annually, dependent on the specific vaccine). However, if a horse sustains a serious injury the vet will give a booster shot, regardless of the horse's vaccination status.

STEP 2

Start to add the Epsom salts, stirring vigorously. Continue to add the salts until no more will dissolve, at which point it is a saturated solution.

STEP 3

Gently lower the horse's foot into the bucket and soak for 15–20 minutes. Repeat according to the vet's instructions.

How to make a soak boot

In some instances it is easier and better to use a soak boot rather than soaking the foot in a bucket, and this alternative can be discussed with the vet.

YOU WILL NEED

Cotton wool
Brown gauze
Duct tape
Self-adhesive bandage
A 60 cc catheter tip syringe

STEP 1

Take a roll of sterile cotton wool and roll it open to a suitable length (this depends on the size of the hoof you are wrapping). Tear the length from the roll then carefully tear it in half along its length. You now have two long, narrow pieces of cotton. Roll these up as if rolling a bandage. This is the easiest way to apply cotton wool to any injury.

STEP 2

Cover the foot and pastern with the cotton wool. Make sure that your wrap is reasonably loose around the pastern area. Secure the cotton wool in place with gauze, and a self-adhesive bandage.

STEP 3

Take the duct tape and totally cover the bandage with strips of the tape. Do not put the tape on tightly over the pastern area. Put several layers of tape in the toe area.

STEP 4

Soak solution can now by siphoned into the boot though the top using a 60 cc catheter tip syringe.   *See photos overleaf* ▶

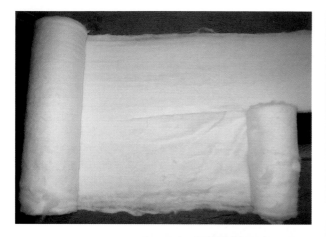

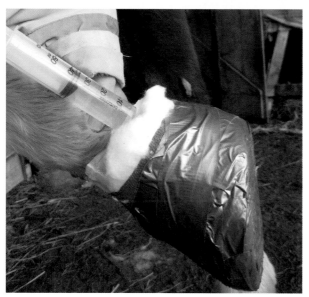

Making a soak boot.

Top left: *Step 1*

Above: *Step 2*

Left: *Step 4*

The horse should be kept in when wearing one of these boots as it will 'walk through' the bandage if moving around.

Alternative soak boots can be make using car inner tubing and duct tape for a more robust boot. They are also available to buy, but are quite costly.

Cracked heels and mud fever

Cracked heels and/or mud fever can be intensely painful and in severe cases cause lameness – in which case the horse should be seen by the vet. The skin at the back of the pasterns and heels (also in some cases of mud fever the backs of the cannon bones and the belly) becomes infected and inflamed. The skin weeps and deep cracks with scabs form. These scabs can be removed using scab softener (see later this chapter) and the skin is then treated with an antibiotic cream such as Dermobian. In less severe cases the skin may be kept soft using udder cream, or a mixture of lanolin and cod liver oil, or a thick-based emollient cream (choose one with a high lipid content).

For non-severe cracked heels try the following salve.

YOU WILL NEED

One jar of petroleum jelly
3 tbsp (45 ml) of olive oil
6 drops of tea tree oil
6 drops of lavender oil
A splash of citronella

STEP **1**

Combine all the ingredients in a clean pan.

STEP **2**

Gently heat and mix thoroughly.

STEP **3**

Pour into a clean receptacle with a lid, allow to cool and keep in a fridge.

Apply to heels every other day.

Thrush

Thrush is an infection that affects the frog, causing it to decompose and form foul-smelling, slimy black matter. The foot needs to be thoroughly scrubbed with water or a solution of water and Betadine (it should be the colour of weak tea), or water and Hibiscrub. Then treat the area with either a weak solution of Betadine or iodine, a spray containing gentian violet or the following anti-thrush spray.

How to make an anti-thrush spray

Make up a mixture made up of one part phenol, to one part 10% formalin and one part iodine. Mix in a spray bottle, label clearly and spray the foot thoroughly. Alternatively, keep in a small bottle with a sponge stopper so the mixture can be applied directly.

(There are a number of ready-made solutions available on the market and, if opting for one of these, consult your veterinary surgeon or farrier first for advice. When treating thrush be careful not to use anything too caustic, which although it might kill the thrush, will also damage the tissue of the frog.)

Alternative thrush treatment

An effective alternative treatment for thrush is to apply a thin layer of sugardine paste to the affected area. Make sugardine by mixing povodine iodine with white sugar or Manuka honey. Start by using 1 part povodine iodine to 2 parts sugar or honey to form a paste. Mix well and assess the consistency. If it is too runny, add more sugar or honey until it thickens, then coat the area. Sugardine is, along with PSS/BET (see How to Make Wound-cleaning spray, later this chapter) one of the most useful items in a first aid kit.

Frog supports for laminitic horses

In severe cases of laminitis where there is pedal bone rotation or sinking, applying homemade frog supports as an emergency first aid procedure can provide *temporary* relief to the horse, though only at the direction of, or on the advice of, the veterinary surgeon.

YOU WILL NEED

Thick polystyrene
Scissors
Duct tape or self-adhesive bandage

STEP 1

Cut two pieces of thick polystyrene large enough to cover the entire frog area and extend back to the heels – approximately 4 x 2 in (10 x 5 cm).

STEP 2

If possible, have the horse standing on a soft surface, which will make it less painful when picking up a foot. Tape each frog support to cover the frog and hold in place using duct tape or self-adhesive bandage. Be prepared before picking the horse's foot up, and tape the supports on as quickly as possible to minimise the amount of time the horse has to hold its foot up, which puts pressure on the other leg.

Alternatively, tape a roll of bandage material (or a piece of folded rubber if you have some to hand) to the underside of the frog.

Tip

Good stable management is the most effective way to prevent thrush occurring.

Dealing with brittle feet

Some horses have particularly poor horn quality in their hooves, which can be slow growing and may be brittle, peel, crack. The fundamental way to address this is to provide the horse with a correctly balanced diet. There are many feed supplements available to help hoof growth which, although expensive, can be very good (Farrier's Formula in particular). These supplements need to contain biotin, methionine, sulphur, choline, magnesium and zinc. Allow at least 3 months on the supplement before noticeable improvement occurs.

Since, as just indicated, poor hoof quality is a problem that needs to be addressed from the inside out, topical applications are generally not effective. They might make the feet look better temporarily, but this is cosmetic rather than a structural effect. There are, however, two products that I have seen noticeable results from: these are Kevin Bacon Hoof Dressing and Cornucrescine.

Wounds

Minor wounds such as scrapes, bruises and cuts can be treated at home, but if in any doubt, if the wound is bleeding profusely, is excessively dirty, is serious or is a puncture wound, then consult the vet.

Making wound treatments

How to make wound-cleaning spray (PSS/BET)

Any open injury should always be carefully cleaned and assessed. If you are going to involve a vet make sure you do not put anything topical on the injury before the vet arrives.

YOU WILL NEED

A gallon (4.5 litre) jug (an old milk container works well)
Distilled water
8 level tsp (40 ml) of salt
8 cc Betadine (povidone-iodine)
Spray bottle

> **Warning**
>
> Puncture wounds may be small, but they can be deadly. Any puncture wound must be seen by the vet.

STEP 1

Fill the jug with distilled water, and label the jug PSS/BET (i.e. saline and Betadine)

STEP 2

Add the 8 tsp (40 ml) of salt.

STEP 3

Add 8 cc Betadine, which will turn the mixture the colour of weak tea, and shake vigorously to mix the ingredients.

STEP 4

Allow to settle and then fill the spray bottle.

This wound-cleaning spray is excellent. It will lose its colour after some time, but is still perfectly good to use. Adjust the spray on the bottle so the mixture is released in a fine spray.

Making saline solution

Simple saline solution can be made by following steps one and two of the above instructions.

How to make scab softener

In some instances it is helpful to apply a scab softener to aid the lifting and removal of scabs, particularly in the case of cracked heels. Bear in mind that conditions/injuries leading to the formation of scabs will invariably be very painful, so use common sense when dealing with the area. Only remove scabs on the advice of the vet.

YOU WILL NEED

One 16 fl oz (0.45 litre) bottle of mineral oil (or baby oil)
One 16 fl oz (0.45 litre) bottle of 3% USP hydrogen peroxide
One ½ fl oz (approx 15 ml) bottle of tincture of iodine
One container

STEP 1

Combine all the ingredients in a large container and mix slowly with a wooden spoon.

Warning

Eye injuries should always be seen by a vet as a matter of urgency. Never wash the eye with saline solution unless under the advice of your vet. Instead wait for the vet to arrive, or follow directions given by the vet over the phone. Keep the horse out of direct light, and quiet.

STEP **2**

The mixture is quite volatile and will bubble and expand. For this reason do not put it in a container with a tightly closed lid until the mixture has settled.

STEP **3**

Apply to the area with care, using either cotton wool, or a sponge stopper.

Proud flesh

Proud flesh or granulation tissue will often form during the healing process of wounds, especially those of the lower leg. This, in moderation, is part of the natural healing process, but sometimes excessive proud flesh forms, which will then cause problems, inhibit the wound from healing and lead to scarring. One of the best ways to prevent proud flesh forming is for the wound to be sutured initially, if possible, and to maintain a really clean and hygienic post-wound care procedure, while also restricting movement of the injury site.

In severe cases where proud flesh has formed the problem will have to be dealt with surgically. In less severe cases it is possible to apply over-the-counter topical applications to the flesh to reduce it. These applications are caustic or burning, so while they might reduce the proud flesh, they do so by destroying the cells, which in turn inhibits healing. Always consult a veterinary surgeon before applying a topical application to a wound.

A traditional remedy is Preparation H, which can help to reduce the flesh and can also encourage the hair to grow back at the injury site.

Scar tissue

The best way to treat scar tissue is to prevent it! One of the best ways to avoid/minimise scarring from injuries is to have the wound sutured as quickly as possible (where possible). In some instances this is impractical and so the wound has to be healed 'open'.

To help healing an open wound:

- Try to minimise the amount of movement the injured area is subjected to.

- Keep the wound as clean and 'healthy' as possible.

- Vitamin E cream is particularly beneficial in aiding wound healing and cutting down on scarring.

Once the wound is healed over, Vaseline or Cornucrescine Intensive Hoof Moisturiser can help to reduce the scarring and encourage hair re-growth.

Scrapes, burns and bruises

For minor scrapes and burns a topical application of sugardine can help with the healing process. Providing the injury is minor, clean it thoroughly with PSS/BET (as described earlier) and then apply a thin layer of sugardine paste.

Arnica

Arnica is one of the most popular herbs used in herbal and homeopathic remedies and has properties said to heal virtually every ill from mental to physical! It has a mild anti-inflammatory effect and is a natural analgesic: true arnica proponents will say it has anti-bacterial properties, but this should be treated with caution. It can be bought in any number of forms from a paste or cream to a liniment or rub, and is also available in an ingestible form. For horses, it is most effective when used for bruises, stiffness and fatigued muscles. However, *never* apply arnica to an open wound.

Bandages and wound dressings

Tip

Electrical tape wrapped over the bandage fastening can help to secure the bandage and prevent it from coming undone.

Self-adhesive bandage material (such as Vetrap) is excellent for veterinary bandaging, but can be expensive. Some brands are marketed as being re-usable, but this rarely works efficiently. This means, in effect, that the bandage material is used once before being discarded. If your horse has an injury that requires bandages to be changed every day, it is easy to see how the costs can escalate. An alternative option is to use tail bandages or similar elasticated bandages, which are washable and of sufficient length. Whenever bandaging, ensure that the pressure is applied evenly, and that the bandage is not pulled too tight, which can lead to circulation problems, sores and chaffing. When applying pressure bandages, and at the vet's directive, make sure that a suitable amount of bandage padding is used, and again that the pressure remains even throughout.

How to make bandages

Bandages can be made for a fraction of the cost for which they can be bought, with fleece travelling or stable bandages being the easiest to make.

The advantage of making your own bandages is primarily that you can fashion them to the exact length you require. It is also a cheaper alternative to buying them, and you have a choice of patterns or colours to use.

For instructions on making travelling/stable bandages see Travelling Bandages in Chapter 2.

Alternative elastic bandage

A really useful way to hold a dressing in place over a knee (which is notoriously difficult to bandage), is to use a human elasticated tubular bandage (Tubigrip). These can be purchased relatively cheaply from any chemist and even the larger supermarkets.

Roll the bandage over the hoof and up the leg, taking care to hold it away from the injury, to above the knee and site of injury. Tape the dressing in place then roll the bandage down and over it. Secure the bandage at the top and bottom with a single layer of sticking plaster.

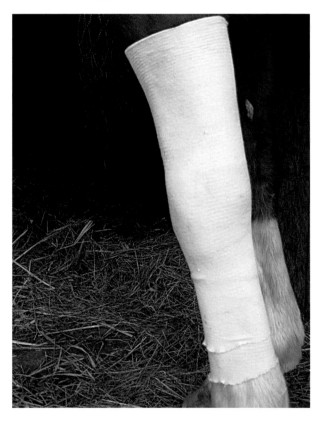

Holding a dressing in place using a Tubigrip bandage.

Alternative bandage padding

A quick and easy way to provide an extra layer of bandage padding for lower leg injuries is to use an old tubular sock. Cut the foot off at the ankle, and if necessary stitch around the bottom to prevent fraying. Apply the wound dressing as directed, hold in place with gauze and then roll the sock material up and over the gauze. A further layer of cotton wool/Gamgee and self-adhesive bandage can then be added over the top.

Tips for veterinary bandaging

- Always use padding such as Gamgee when applying a bandage.

- Use recycled plastic bags or Clingfilm (US Saran wrap) to cover poultices or sweats. This helps to keep the heat/cold in, and prevents the bandage from becoming wet and possibly tightening.

- When starting a bandage, turn the top corner of the bandage down and over the first pass, and then bandage over it; this helps to keep the bandage secure.

- Traditionally, bandages are applied from below the knee down the leg and then back up again to encourage swelling to dissipate. However bandaging from the bottom of the leg up to the knee and back down provides a more secure bandage that is less likely to slip.

- Disposable nappies make good hoof bandages.

- Secure bandages with a single pass of robust sticking plaster around the top and bottom of the bandage.

- Never leave bandages on for longer than 12 hours (unless at a veterinary surgeon's directive).

- Do not try to re-use self-adhesive bandage material, it does not work.

- Tail bandages can be useful for bandaging legs instead of using self-adhesive bandages (which are expensive), but be careful that they are not pulled too tight or positioned over the tendons or on the inside of the leg.

- Sanitary towels can be used as wound dressings if no commercial dressing is available.

- Sanitary towels are also suitable to be used on eye injuries, at the directive of a veterinary surgeon.

- Packing tape/duct tape is excellent for bolstering hoof bandages and much cheaper than proprietary sticking plaster.

- Gamgee and cotton wool padding should not be re-used as the fibres settle and become uneven, which leads to uneven bandage pressure.

- Some mares have a tendency to become very dirty under their tails. If this is the case use warm water with a little baby oil in it to clean the area up and keep the skin soft.

Dealing with eye injuries

All eye injuries must be seen by the vet as a matter of urgency: never treat an eye injury with a topical application before it has been seen by the vet, unless the vet has instructed you to do so over the phone. Generally eye injuries are not bandaged, but if for some reason one needs to be, human sanitary towels (un-perfumed) can be useful dressings, since the towels are a suitable shape and provide good padding. If possible, try to moisten the pad with a little saline solution or commercial eyewash. The pad can be held in place with Vetrap and adhesive bandage.

Because of their size and padded quality, sanitary towels are also useful for other small injuries.

Holding eye dressings in place

Vetrap or similar elasticated bandage material can be used in conjunction with adhesive bandage to secure the padding and bandage. Run the bandage across the padding and eye, between the ears and under the jaw.

Another way of securing an eye bandage is using a pair of tights. Take a large pair of elasticated tights and cut off both legs to leave one large hole. Just below the waistband area cut out two holes, through which the ears will be threaded, and further down cut another hole for the unaffected eye. Slide the doctored tights up over the nose, waistband first, and thread the ears through the holes. (It might be necessary to make a slit in the tights under the jaw in the throat-latch area.) The whole bandage can be further secured by sticking plaster if necessary. *See photos overleaf* ▶

Insects and itchiness

Flies and other insects can be a real nuisance for horses and, in some cases, may contribute to the incidence of various diseases. There are various management practices that can help reduce these problems, including the following.

- Using fly sheets when turning out is a big advantage, or changing routines to turn out at night instead of during the heat of the day makes sense.

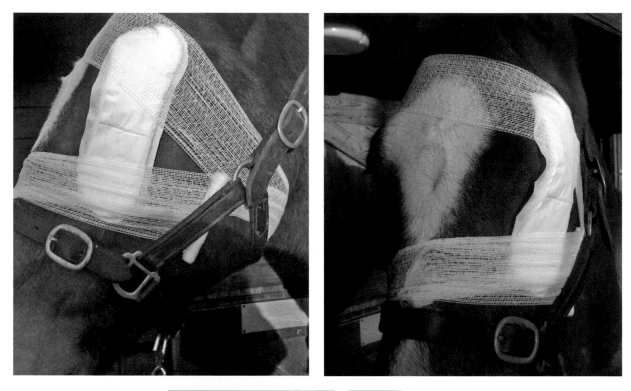

Methods for holding eye dressings in place.

- Try to keep muck heaps away from stables and pastures; keep muck picked up and avoid having containers of stagnant water around the place.

- Hanging sticky fly strips, which are inexpensive, in the stables, tack and feed room is good, but make sure they are hung high enough to prevent walking into them!

Homemade fly repellents

There are innumerable insect repellents on the market, some of which are very expensive and only some of which are effective. There are several home-made recipes for combating flies, which are much cheaper than store-bought brands. These do work but, again are not totally effective; the advantage with them is that they are economical and that the ingredients are natural and non-caustic.

Some key constituents

Garlic

The beneficial properties of garlic, both for humans and equines, has long been recognised. It is most commonly fed to horses in powdered or granule form and acts as a natural fly/insect repellent, as well as being good for general digestion. Garlic is also said to promote a healthy urinary tract, to be good for blood pressure, to work as an anti-inflammatory and to aid the efficiency of the respiratory tract. Always follow the recommended dose according to the manufacturer.

Vinegar

A capful of white vinegar in the horse's drinking water can help repel flies, but make sure that the taste of the vinegar is not putting the horse off its water. Vinegar is also a prime ingredient for home made fly-repellents, see below.

Vaseline

Some horses are particularly sensitive to flies around their ears. Try smearing a thin layer of Vaseline on the inside of the top of each ear; this prevents the flies from landing there and can help cut down on the irritation factor.

How to make fly repellent

There are several different recipes for fly spray and below are a couple of the more effective ones. *Always* do a test patch before dousing the horse with the spray to make sure it does not react to any of the ingredients. To do a test patch, spray the fly repellent on a tiny area of the shoulder and leave for 24 hours. If a reaction occurs wash off immediately with warm water.

The basic ingredients for homemade fly sprays are most often a combination of the following:

- Avon Skin so Soft bath oil or Skin so Soft dry oil body spray
- White vinegar
- Tea (chamomile)
- Citronella oil
- Lavender oil
- Tea tree oil
- Eucalyptus oil
- Polysorbate 20

Recipe 1

8 fl oz (0.23 litre) of water
8 fl oz (0.23 litre) of Skin so Soft bath oil
1 lb (0.45 kg) white vinegar
1 tbsp (15 ml) eucalyptus oil
1tbsp (15 ml) polysorbate 20
4 drops of citronella

Mix all the ingredients together and keep in a labelled spray bottle.

Recipe 2

16 fl oz (0.45 litre) cold tea
16 fl oz (0.45 litre) apple cider vinegar (or white vinegar)
20 drops eucalyptus oil
20 drops citronella oil
10 drops lavender oil
10 drops tea tree oil
20 drops polysorbate 20

Mix all the ingredients together and keep in a labelled spray bottle.

Recipe 3

8 fl oz (0.23 litre) cold tea
8 fl oz (0.23 litre) Skin so Soft bath oil

Tip

Polysorbate 20 is an emulsifier that acts to dissolve oils in water. It is a useful addition to the other products because it allows the essential oils to dissolve properly and therefore they are more evenly dispersed. Repellents using essential oils can be made without the addition of an emulsifier but will need to be shaken vigorously before use. Polysorbate is reasonably priced, and can be easily obtained online and in some health food shops.

16 fl oz (0.45 litre) white vinegar
20 drops lavender oil
20 drops polysorbate 20
4 cloves of garlic

Crush the garlic and add to the tea while still hot. Add the remaining ingredients, stir well and allow to steep overnight. Strain the juice to remove the garlic remnants and decant into a labelled spray bottle.

Insect salves

Some horses are particularly sensitive to insect bites, and using one of the following can help to take away the sting or itch.

Anti-itch paste 1

Mix a little meat tenderiser with water to make a paste and apply to the bite or sting.

Anti-itch paste 2

Mix baking soda with apple cider vinegar to make a paste and apply to the bite or sting.

Vinegar

Dab vinegar onto the bite or sting to take away the itch and help reduce inflammation.

Other topical applications

Try dabbing a drop of either witch hazel, lavender or tea tree oil directly on the bite to reduce itching and swelling.

Anti-itch spray

Many horses will start to rub their mane and tail in the spring as the midges and flies start to show. Providing this (and not sweet itch) is the cause then applying an anti-itch and conditioning spray to the crest and dock areas can help.

YOU WILL NEED

A labelled spray bottle
2 pints (1.14 litres) water
2 tbsp (30 ml) baby oil
2 tbsp (30 ml) Skin so Soft bath oil
4 tbsp (60 ml) Listerine original mouthwash

> **Caution**
>
> Word of warning with the tea – very strong tea will stain greys, so if you have a grey or a light-coloured horse then use a weak tea mix, or replace the tea with half water and half white vinegar.

Mix all the ingredients together and store in a spray bottle. The oil in the mixture helps to keep the hairs conditioned, the Skin so Soft is a natural fly repellent and the Listerine helps to reduce the itch. Apply liberally twice a day or as needed.

Oral medications and how to 'cheat'

Some horses can be notoriously difficult to administer oral medication to, but there are a few ways to 'cheat'.

Get the horse used to taking medications orally by using a syringe. Mix a little molasses with water and administer to the horse on a regular basis (a couple of times a week). Most horses will grow to love the taste of molasses and will actively seek the syringe. Once they have been taught that this is a good thing, antibiotic powders can then be mixed with the molasses and given orally. If the horse is used to having a syringe inserted in the corner of the mouth, it makes giving worming paste much easier as well.

As an alternative, get the horse used to apple sauce and use this to disguise oral medications.

If a horse will not accept a syringe in its mouth and it is causing more distress to continue trying, then mix medications with a small amount of molasses (or honey) and place inside a hollowed out apple or carrot.

Having checked the labelling to ensure that there is no problem with storage at a low temperature, keep wormers in the fridge for two days prior to administering, as this reduces the smell. They can then be added to the food, or administered as outlined above.

Encouraging a horse to drink

It is absolutely essential that horses drink a sufficient amount, and their water intake should, where possible, always be monitored.

- Make sure water receptacles are clean and scrub them out on a regular basis. Do not use detergents or soaps to clean buckets; if necessary use baking soda.

- Provide the horse with a salt block at all times and keep the block clean. Either hang it using a piece of hosepipe and baling twine, or place on the ground in a bucket.

- In the winter, if the water becomes very chilled, either add warm water to make the temperature more moderate, or invest in a water heater (particularly relevant in very cold climates).

- Often horses will only drink their 'own' water. If this is the case, when travelling with your horse take enough water with you to last the duration of the trip.

- On a similar note, it can be helpful to adapt a horse to drinking flavoured water. Add a little apple juice or cordial to the water at home to get your horse used to the flavour; this flavoured water can then be used to disguise electrolytes, should you need to administer them. This can also be helpful when travelling: if it is not possible to take enough water with you for the duration of the trip, you can disguise 'foreign' water by adding the juice or cordial.

- Horses in hard work, especially in hot temperatures, and those travelling on long journeys, may well require the addition of electrolytes to their diet. First consult a vet as incorrect/inappropriate administration can be counter-productive. There are a number of different ways electrolytes may be administered including as a paste, powder or granules, and added to the feed, the water or given orally.

- To encourage a horse to drink immediately, try mixing a teaspoon (5 ml) of table salt in some apple sauce, then administer orally through a syringe and provide the horse with a fresh bucket of water. The salt will normally persuade the horse to drink within a couple of minutes.

- Another trick is to administer 5 cc (roughly 1 teaspoon) of corn syrup orally. This very sweet and sticky substance will generally encourage the horse to drink; after administering, provide the horse with a bucket of fresh water.

- Use sloppy sugar beet, or add a generous amount of water to the horse's feeds to top up its fluid intake.

- Similarly, feed soaked hay and succulents where appropriate.

Miscellaneous useful remedies

Anti-chew treatments

Some horses are notorious chewers. First address the cause, which is often boredom, and try to alleviate this through exercise, turning out and providing stimulation in the form of company.

Horses that by necessity and for whatever reason need to be kept on their own can be helped through providing them with a mirror in the stable. Only use specialist equine mirrors, which cannot shatter, or plastic acrylic mirrors, which also will not shatter. Specific equine ones are generally not cheap, but studies have shown that they do provide the horse with some level of comfort.

There are a number of expensive anti-chew/cribbing products on the market, which are pretty effective. However, equally good are some home-made remedies, which might have to be re-applied several times until the horse gets the message.

- A permanent remedy is to cover the chewed area with a metal strip – particularly relevant for stable doors and gate tops.

- Treating all wooden areas such as stables and fences with creosote used to be an excellent method of preserving the wood and preventing the horse from chewing it. This is now no longer available in the UK, although similar, less caustic, products are. It is expensive to treat wood with these products, but is worth it as a long-term investment. It will greatly increase the natural life of the wooden structures and keep them from being chewed.

Vaseline, cayenne pepper and hot sauce

Mix a generous amount of cayenne pepper, tabasco, chilli seeds or any other fiery substance with Vaseline and apply a thin layer to the areas that are being chewed.

Alternatively, take any store-bought hot sauce, the hotter the better, and apply a thin layer to the area being chewed. This will stop most horses in their tracks, though it has to be said that a few horses seem to have developed a taste for it!

Healthy coats

An old-fashioned, but very effective way to promote a healthy coat is to feed linseed as a supplement, but be warned that it will also put condition on, so it is not suitable for horses/ponies that are prone to being overweight. Linseed is the seed of the flax plant, and in its natural state is extremely poisonous. It must be properly prepared before being fed to the horse. Traditionally raw linseed could be bought; it was then necessary to soak it overnight (at least 12 hours) before boiling it for 5–10 minutes and simmering until a jelly formed. It is then allowed to cool and had to be fed within 12 hours, or else it became rancid. Now it is possible to buy linseed ready prepared, which makes it much more convenient to use. *Always feed linseed supplement in accordance with the manufacturer's guidelines.*

Tired rider's muscles

At the end of a long day in the saddle there is nothing quite so relaxing as a mustard bath. Run a bath and add a generous amount (3–4 tbsp/about 50 ml) of English mustard powder and several drops of eucalyptus oil, lavender oil or tea tree oil. The relaxing effects of a mustard bath are increased by consumption of an alcoholic restorative and a big slice of fruit cake!

CHAPTER 6

Yard equipment

There are a number of ways to cut down on the cost of yard equipment, and to make the yard routine easier. So much of it boils down to personal habit and ease of equipment. Cross-ties, for example, are one of the greatest additions to any suitable yard or barn, and can be made cheaply and easily.

Sometimes money can be saved simply by buying generic items from shops other than specific tack shops. For example forks, buckets, water containers and other items can often be picked up more cheaply from hardware shops or builders' merchants than from tack shops, while items such as the ubiquitous spray bottle (absolutely essential yard equipment) can on occasion be found in discount stores. Sponges, clothes and storage crates can all be bought very cheaply from discount shops, and it is definitely always worth doing some price-checking (if you have time!) before making purchases.

Securing horses

Cross-ties

Horses should be introduced to cross-ties with caution if they are unused to being secured in this way, but generally it takes only a short time to accustom the horse to this method of tying up, and allows the handler greater speed and ease when working around the animal.

Cross-ties can either be situated within indoor barns on either side of the aisle, or can be used in traditional stables.

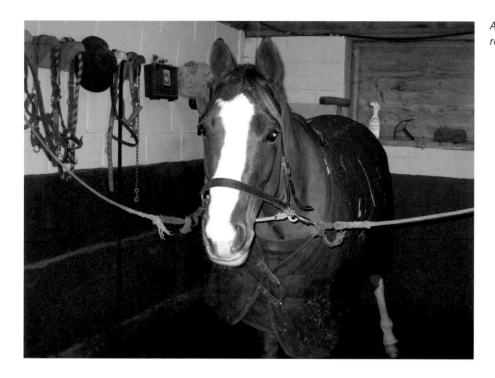

How to make cross-ties

YOU WILL NEED

Two metal rings on plates
Two lengths of chain or rope, length dependent on the area they are to span
Four spring clips (snaps US)
Two pieces of baling twine

STEP 1

Position the two rings one on either side of the stable or aisle. The rings need to be at least 5½ ft (1.68 m) from the floor, and the same height on both sides.

STEP 2

When purchasing the chain, be aware of the weight. You want a heavy enough link to be durable, without being excessively heavy. Use common sense and consider the size and stamp of horse. Attach a regular spring clip to one end of each piece of chain. You have several options on the other end of the chain, which is the end that will attach to the headcollar. Either you can tie a short piece of baling twine – approximately 3 in (7.5 cm) to the chain and attach a regular spring clip to this, or you can attach a quick-release clip to the chain itself.

Using baling twine to attach the spring clip to the chain.

STEP 3

If the cross-ties are to be used in the stable itself, always unclip the chain and remove it from the stable after use, to prevent any chance of an accident. If, however, they are to be used in the aisle of a barn or in a washstand, they can be left attached to the wall rings.

Metal cross-ties can be quite noisy, especially when attached to an impatient horse. If the noise is distracting then buy a length of soft rubber pipe (available from most hardware/DIY shops), or use an old bicycle inner tube. Tie a piece of baling twine through the end of the chain and feed the twine through the pipe/tube. You can then pull the chain through and get rid of the twine. This will, however, increase your cost.

Trailer ties

When travelling, some people prefer to use trailer ties instead of tying the horse up with its lead rope. The advantage of trailer ties is that they can remain in the trailer and are quick and easy to use, and are the correct length. They also reduce the chance of an escape artist horse managing to untie itself during transit. Basically, trailer ties are made along the same principles as cross-ties, the exception being that trailer ties should have quick-release clips on both ends so that, in the case of a serious accident, it is always possible to release the horse. If using a length of chain it should be encased in rubber as described above, or else you can use rope, with a rope clamp and quick-release clips. Some trailer ties available on the market are a thick rubber bungee cord. I suggest avoiding elastic ties as most horses quickly figure out that they give when pulled against, which can increase the chance of accident.

Leave trailer ties in the trailer or lorry so they are ready for use, but always unclip the horse's lead rope after leading it into the vehicle, and do not leave the rope dangling.

Stall guards

Stall guards can be quite useful: compared to a stable door they let extra light and air into a stable, and they can be especially useful for horses that are kept in for long periods. They should, however, be treated with caution. Some horses can be encouraged to try escaping when faced with a stall guard instead of the customary door, so be warned! Webbing or canvas guards are relatively inexpensive to buy. They can also be made and are, in fact, a simple design, but the main drawback in making them is ensuring that the webbing and stitching used are strong enough to contain a horse. With this in mind, better options are either to buy one, or to make your own chain guard. Alternatively you can make a 'slip rail' using a suitably sized piece of timber – 2 x 4 in (5 x 10 cm), which can be slid across the front of the door opening on the inside of the stable.

How to make a chain stall guard

YOU WILL NEED

A length of middleweight chain, length dependent on width of door
A piece of flexible rubber tubing large enough to accommodate the chain
Two spring clips
Two metal screw-in eyelets with a long thread*

*These will need to be screwed into stout timber if they are going to do the job. If the timber available to fix them into is of only moderate thickness, it is probably better to use eyelets based on metal studding, and fix this right through the stable wall, securing with washers and nuts.

STEP **1**

Measure the width of the doorway and make allowances for the eyelets and the spring clips. The chain needs to rest with just a slight bow in it. Make sure it is not too loose. Tie a piece of baling twine through the end link of chain and thread through the rubber pipe, then pull the chain through the pipe and remove the string.

STEP **2**

Attach the spring clips one to each end of the chain and screw the eyelets into the doorframe. They need to be just marginally below the level of where the top of the stable door would be.

Dealing with banging, scraping and boredom

Banging

There are few things more irritating than a horse that repeatedly kicks its stable door or the side of the trailer or lorry, or scrapes and paws the ground by the stable door. Although it is virtually impossible to completely eliminate this habit once started, it is possible to help minimise it. One of the main ways is to deaden the noise, as some horses seem to relish the noise, and the subsequent attention that the habit generates.

Stable doors

For the horse that repeatedly kicks its stable door, buy a thick doormat and fasten it to the inside bottom of the door, using twin-thread screws. Sometimes this actively discourages the horse from kicking the door; if not it at least deadens the noise and offers the door some protection. Alternatively, and often more expensively, you can fix rubber sheeting to the inside of the door.

Trailers and lorries

Many vehicles are now supplied with matting partially lining the walls. However, if this is not the case with your vehicle, and the horse is belting the sides, then try attaching either door mats or rubber in the appropriate places (including the partitions if necessary).

Scraping the floor

A horse scraping the floor in front of the stable door, especially before feeding time, is not uncommon. To cut down on the noise and wear and tear try laying a rubber stable mat (although these are expensive). Some horses will stop pawing if they are restrained by a stall guard instead of a door (only do this during the day and only when people are around). If you decide to try this, make sure the guard will confine the horse, and that the stable is in a secure yard, should the horse escape. Try keeping the horse turned out as much as possible, feed hay in nets with small holes, that require some effort and time to eat, and be aware of the activity in rest of the yard (e.g. don't leave the horse in its stable if all the others are turned out or being ridden out).

Bear in mind that horses bang and kick for a reason, often boredom, nervousness or excitement. Try to address the root cause of the problem and solve it if possible.

Stable diversions

Some horses find stable toys an entertaining diversion, especially if they are on box rest, or stabled for long periods. There are a number of different ways to provide diversions in the stable, but here are a few ideas.

Mirrors

Studies have shown that some horses can really benefit from a mirror in the stable; in particular this has been shown to reduce weaving in horses. Specific horse mirrors can be bought, or you can purchase your own sheet of acrylic mirror for a lot less money. Seek out plastics companies, of which there are many on the internet.

When installing a mirror in the stable make sure that it is not in an position whereby the horse will see its own reflection close up when eating. The horse must also be able to 'escape' the reflection. Generally, if the mirror is installed just inside the stable door on the wall and at head height it works well.

A few horses will have an adverse and aggressive reaction to a mirror so be aware when installing one.

If you purchase a sheet of acrylic plastic yourself then screw it to the wall and cover the edge with trim, also screwed to the wall.

Hanging toys

Hanging diversions are appreciated by some horses. Try tying an old plastic cordial bottle or milk jug so that it dangles either in a corner of the stable or to the edge of the doorway opening, to give the horse something to bash around. Tie it so that the bottle/jug is approximately at eye level, or slightly lower. Remove any lid and labels before tying and use only large, sturdy bottles or jugs. If the horse actually gets hold of and crushes the item, as some will, then remove and replace with a new one. You can put a few small pebbles in the bottle/jug, since some horses like the sound they make, or add a little water so the item has some weight to it.

Some horses love turnips and swedes. Punch a hole through the vegetable then string a loop of baling twine through it and tie up as detailed above. The horse will try to chomp the vegetable and while away hours attempting to get hold of it. (Be careful about the size of the vegetable, though. An acquaintance of the editor gave his wind-sucking horse a large turnip to play with. The horse attempted to take a bite out of it, but it was just too big and 'pinged' out of his jaws. It then swung back and clonked him between the eyes, like a scene from a Tom and Jerry cartoon.)

Many horses are happier peering out over the stable door, so keep this in mind and place the toy to the front of the stable.

Balls

While many horses will ignore a ball, some do play actively with them. There are a number of specific horse balls on the market, and other similar toys that can also be filled with treats that trickle out to encourage the horse to move them around. However, if you don't want to splash out on a toy that might not be appreciated, try using an old basketball, netball or football (ask at local schools or gyms to see if they have any old ones they are getting rid of, or check for suitably sized balls in the local discount store).

Diversions in water tanks

Try placing one or two apples in your horse's water bucket. This works best in round buckets as opposed to square waterers. The horse will attempt to bob for the apples. This is also a good way to keep buckets clear of ice in the winter.

Keeping water buckets ice-free

In very cold weather one of the only ways to keep buckets free of ice is through the use of either heated tanks or heating elements. However extreme weather in the UK (as compared to the US) is both relatively uncommon and short-lived. To prevent thin ice forming on water buckets and tanks during moderately cold weather try, as mentioned above, placing one or two apples in the water bucket to help keep the water moving around. Alternatively, place a buoyant ball in the bucket, which will also help to prevent icing over.

Making equipment for the yard

Bucket covers

Bucket covers are really useful. Although relatively cheap to buy, they are very easy to make, so if you do have some material lying around that can be put to use then it is worth making your own.

YOU WILL NEED

A piece of material that is at least 6 in (15 cm) wider than the diameter of the bucket

A piece of elastic a little over half the circumference of the bucket in length

A large safety pin

Needle, thread and pins

STEP 1

The easiest way to measure the material is to place the bucket upside down on the material and trace around the edge. Remove the bucket and draw a second line allowing at least an extra 3 in (7.5 cm) margin all the way round. Cut the material out (it is helpful to use cotton or a material that is easy to wash) and pin a hem all the way around the edge, but leave a small gap to pass the elastic through.

Making a bucket cover.
Step 1

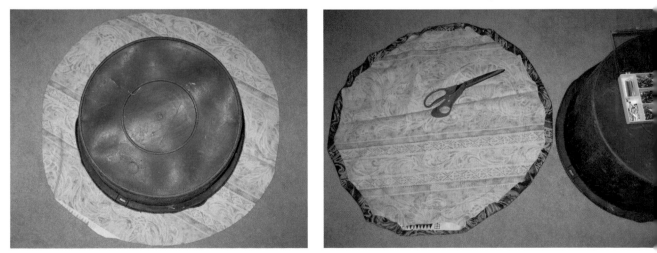

STEP 2

Stitch the hem then attach the safety pin to one end of the elastic and push it through the hem. Stitch the two ends of the elastic together and then sew up the hole in the hem.

Step 2

The finished cover.

Feed scoops

Feed scoops are easily made from old milk jugs, or a simple empty coffee can. Always feed by weight though, and never by the 'can' or the scoop unless you have pre-weighed the feed and know exactly how much each can or scoop contains nutritionally.

To make a scoop from an old milk jug, mark where indicated in the photo and then cut along the line. If the edges are too sharp then line them with electrical tape. Small milk jugs can be useful measures for supplements.

Haynets

It is quite possible to make your own haynet using old baling twine, a bit of patience and some ingenuity. The cost of new haynets is relatively low, so to make your own, although free, does require a certain amount of time! It is, however, the perfect job to entertain young helpers around the yard. Assemble 24 pieces of baling twine and tie together in one knot. The easiest way to tie the net is to dangle the pieces of joined string from a ceiling hook (bridle peg) or similar. Work your way around, tying each piece of string to the next, then alternate on the next row down. When you near the end of the twine, knot the top of each piece to leave a loop. Take another piece of twine and thread through the loops to form the tying section.

(Baling twine is also useful for mending rips and tears in haynets, or for replacing their tie-strings.)

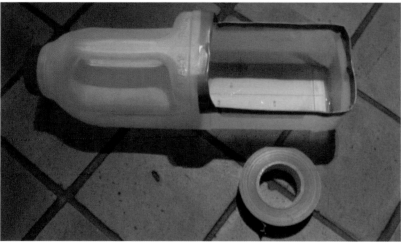

The three stages of making a feed scope from a milk container.

Humper-dumpers

Humper-dumpers are one of the most useful items to have around the place, and are easily and cheaply made. You can make them any size to suit, but a good general size is 5½ or 6 ft (1.7 or 1.83 m) square. They can be used for moving just about anything from loose bedding to hay to tack and blankets, or can be used on top of a full barrow to prevent bits flying round the place.

YOU WILL NEED

A square of heavy cotton or canvas material of up to 6 ft (1.83 m)
Four 18 in (45 cm) pieces of webbing

STEP **1**

Stitch a 1 in (2.5 cm) hem all the way around the piece of material.

STEP 2

If using the webbing, tack each piece to the corners to form the handles, then stitch securely in place using a square formation with a crossed diagonal pattern to stitch.

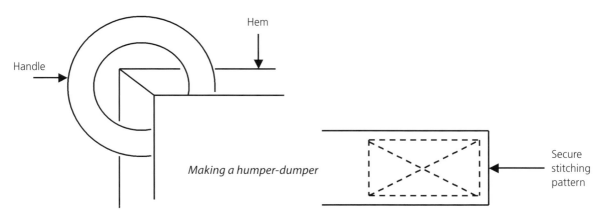

Handle

Hem

Making a humper-dumper

Secure stitching pattern

Nameplates and feeding instructions

There is no denying that brass nameplates and fancy stud card holders do look lovely on the outside of the stable, but they are expensive. An alternative way to provide information such as the horse's name and feeding requirements is to print the information onto a piece of paper and laminate it. Laminating is pretty inexpensive and should remain waterproof for some time. To perk up a laminated sheet, nail a border of thin wooden trim (treat with weatherproofing first) to the outside perimeter.

Storage

A sensible system of storage around the yard makes all the difference, both to ease and accessibility and to the care of the items. 'Storage' covers a huge range, from feed and hay to tack, blankets and accessories, and in all cases it is a question of finding what works for your situation and what is the most cost-effective approach.

Pallets

Hay should always be stored on pallets to lift it off the ground and to help cut down on the possibility of mould. Pallets are invaluable to have around the place, for storing not just hay and sacks of feed, but anything that needs to

Laundry baskets

Cheap plastic laundry baskets make excellent mucking out skips, and can often be found in the discount stores or picked up for very little in hardware shops.

be kept from the ground. Occasionally it is possible to get used pallets from feed merchants, timber yards and building merchants for next to nothing, and it is always worth asking. If you have pallets, never throw them away, even if they are broken; they can generally be mended easily. There are also companies that specialise in buying and selling pallets, and if you have to buy some, always go for recycled ones and check on the internet for suppliers.

Large containers

Feeds need to be stored in vermin-proof containers. Old chest freezers make excellent storage for grain and feeds, and can invariably be picked up second-hand for next to nothing. Dustbins with lids also work well, and are easy to clean and hose out – try to buy ones made from recycled plastic. Dustbins are also useful for soaking haynets in, and can be easily tipped over to drain.

If storing feeds in containers, make sure that the lids and containers are clearly marked so there is no confusion over the feedstuff within (i.e. between things such as horse and pony cubes and unsoaked sugar beet pellets). It is preferable to store the feed still in its bag in the container rather than emptying the contents out. If you do empty the contents into the container, then the container must be thoroughly cleaned out and dried regularly to prevent the build-up of old, dusty and stale feedstuffs at the bottom.

Other storage items

Storage boxes

Recycled plastic storage boxes are very useful: they come with snap-on lids, are vermin-proof and easy to clean. Storing blankets, numnahs, boots and accessories in boxes helps to preserve them and keep them clean. Label boxes on the outside and store products with mothballs! (Although it is possible to make your own wooden storage boxes, the actual cost of buying the wood exceeds that of purchasing recycled plastic boxes.)

Old school trunks and metal army trunks are also excellent for storing blankets, and can be found in second-hand shops, on eBay or in army surplus stores.

Tool kit boxes available from any big DIY shops make excellent grooming kit boxes, and are often considerably cheaper than specific equestrian grooming boxes. When looking for suitable grooming boxes always go for one with a lid; open boxes get full of dirt and dust, and there is the danger of losing bits and pieces from them.

Milk crates

These are wonderful to have around the yard, though they can be relatively difficult to track down now unless you have an obliging milkman. Use milk crates for setting soaked haynets on to allow excess water to dissipate: they are useful for storing bandages and as jump fillers. One of their most useful aspects regarding storage is they are stackable and fit neatly one on top of the other.

How to make a whip holder

Whips – particularly long dressage whips or lunge whips – are often subject to damage. An easy way to organise and protect your whips is to use several lengths of plastic plumbing pipe, exterior waste pipe, or soil pipe being the best diameters. You can alter the directions that follow to suit the amount or type of whips you have.

YOU WILL NEED
A 3¼ ft (1 m) length of 3 in (7.5 cm) diameter pipe
A 2 ft 6 in (76 cm) length of pipe
An 18 in (45 cm) piece of pipe
Four plastic cable ties

STEP **1**
Ask at a local plumbing supply shop to see if they have any off-cuts of a suitable length or else purchase the lengths that you need. Take the four cable ties and attach them together in pairs so you have two long cable ties.

STEP **2**
Wrap one tie around the top of the three lengths of pipe and one around the bottom to join them together.

If the holder is unstable you can always attach a small bracket to the back and fix to the wall. Alternatively build a wooden triangle into which the holder will fit, which will further stabilise it.

How to make a bootjack

There is nothing worse than struggling to pull muddy boots off, hopping around on one leg, or trying pull one boot off with the other one, which is bad for the heels. (If your boots are tight, it is also a good way to pull your

> ### Tip
> To help preserve the life of lunge whips, wrap duct tape or sticking plaster around the whip at the point where the thong joins the stock.

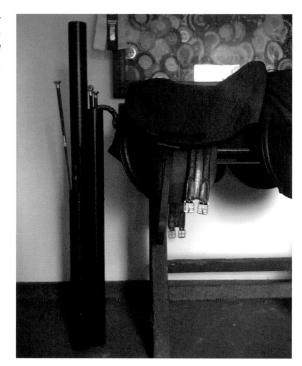

A whip holder is handy for preventing whips being lost or trampled underfoot.

calf muscle!) Bootjacks are easy and cheap to make, particularly if you have off-cuts of old pieces of wood lying around the place, which many yards seem to!

YOU WILL NEED

One piece of plywood (or something similar) 13 x 6 x ¾ in (33 x 15 x 2 cm)

One piece of dowel 5 x 1 in (12.5 x 2.5 cm)

Two screws (these will need to resist quite a lot of force and should therefore be nearly – but not as – long as the combined thickness of the pieces of wood they are joining)

Drill, drill bit

Saw

STEP 1

If you wish, you can taper your piece of wood so it is 6 in (15 cm) wide at the 'boot' end and approximately 4 in (10 cm) at the other end: although it is not necessary, this does look better!

STEP 2

Cut a triangular section from the wide end of the wood. This needs to be about 4 in (10 cm) wide and approximately 4 in (10 cm) deep or, to be more precise, just slightly larger than the outline of your booted foot. If you have access to a jigsaw, you can cut out a rounded section that mirrors this outline quite accurately.

STEP 3

Measure 6 in (15 cm) from the wide end of the wood (the front of the jack) and draw a line. This is where the dowel will be attached to the underside. Pre-drill two holes in the wood, and two holes in the dowel, then screw the dowel to the wood. You now have a bootjack!

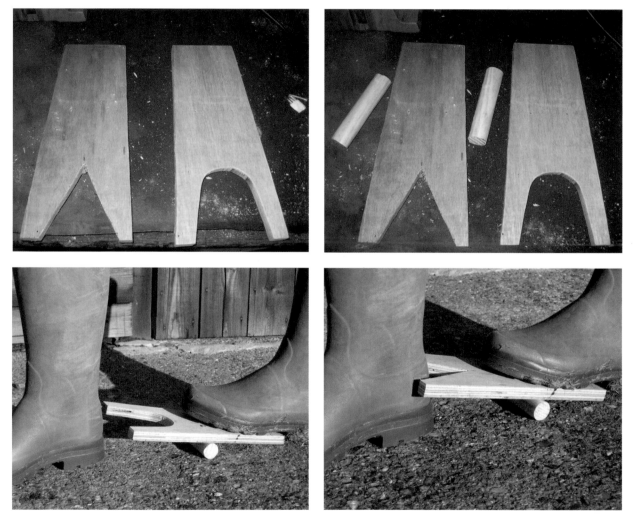

The stages of making a boot jack.

How to make a boot rack

A boot rack is a great way to store wellies and rubber boots (though never your leather dressage boots!), keeping them out of the way, clean and allowing the boots to dry.

YOU WILL NEED

Two pieces of wood 2½ x 1½ x 30 in (6.5 x 3.8 x 76 cm)
Two pieces of 2½ x 1.5 x 12 in (6.3 x 3.8 x 30 cm)
6 Six pieces of dowel 1 x 18 in (2.5 x 45 cm)
Eight 2 in (5 cm) screws
Six 1½ in (3.8 cm) screws
Drill, drill bit and flat wood bit

STEP 1

Take the two long pieces of wood and mark with a dot 3¾ in (9.5 cm) from one end on each piece. This will be the centre of the first hole. Then mark 12½ in (32 cm) from the end on each piece, and finally 21¾ in (55 cm).

STEP 2

Using the marks as the centre of your holes, now drill to a depth of 1 in (2.5 cm). You should now have two pieces of wood, each with three 1 in (2.5 cm) holes in them.

STEP 3

Turn one of the pieces the other way so that the holes are not opposite each other. Next, position the short pieces of wood at either end. These will be screwed onto the underneath of the two long pieces. Pre-drill the screw holes to prevent the wood from splitting then screw the short pieces to the long pieces using the 2 in (5 cm) screws, two in each corner.

STEP 4

Now pre drill your screw holes in the bottom of each piece of dowel and through the bottom of the holes in the long pieces of wood, then screw the dowel in place.

See photos overleaf ▶

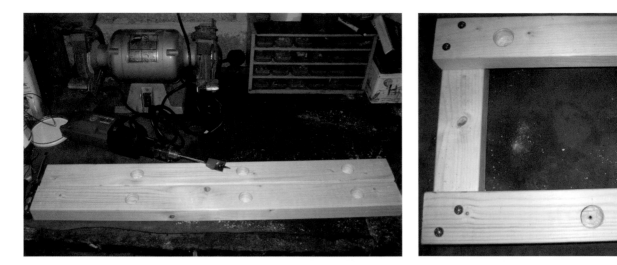

Photos show the stages of making a boot rack.

The finished rack.

CHAPTER 7

Stable management

Environmental considerations

Remarkably, there are very few publications solely devoted to eco-friendly *and* economical stable management practices in the UK. The US boasts a rather more obvious environmentally friendly sector of the equine industry, which includes a number of companies that specifically deal in nothing other than eco-aware equestrian products. While there *are* UK companies that have addressed this, and do market and sell these types of products, they don't appear to have the web space or media coverage that their US contemporaries do. The horse industry continues to thrive, despite a fluctuating financial market, and remains often highly and surprisingly divorced from 'green' credentials at its foundations. Although there are lots of people who are running eco-friendly yards and doing their bit, as an industry in its entirety, there needs to be a more concerted effort across the board to encourage a more environmentally healthy approach to horse husbandry and practices.

Having said this, considerations of economy are also always at the forefront of any equestrian household, and there are, unfortunately, cases where the 'green' alternative works out more expensive. It is at this point that personal ethics and the bank account have to reach some degree of balance and agreement. In some instances an initial higher outlay of cash will eventually turn around to work out more economical in the long run, a classic example being the installation of solar panels. These have already decreased in price recently (do some research and shop around) and will, over time, significantly reduce the amount of grid energy used. Although, in the UK, it is virtually unheard of to heat American-style horse barns, in the US where the climate can be considerably colder it is fairly common, and solar panels come into their own. In the UK, solar panels are useful for heating water for washing down horses or for taking the chill off tack rooms. Solar panels on a smaller scale can be used for powering electric fencing. (Before investing in solar-powered electric fencing, make sure that the unit will provide enough power to cope with the length of fencing you have and, if possible, keep a charged spare battery as back-up.)

Eco-friendly

Eco-friendly: what does it really mean? Well, it *should* mean that the product has been produced with as little damage as possible to the environment, but it is a term that is not regulated and is currently being used by companies to attract a wider market. Foods that claim to be organic are regulated, but other products that state their 'greenness' are not subject to legislation. Be warned that when buying a product that claims to be eco-friendly that it might not be as 'green' as you think. Do try to research a little bit and find out if it really is coming from a sustainable or renewable source or meets with its other alleged 'green' points.

Going 'green' around the yard

Unfortunately it is rare to have either the opportunity, or the money, to build the 'ideal' yard from scratch, so inevitably one is left working with existing structures. This can present certain hurdles when trying to set up and run an eco-friendly yard, but nothing is ever impossible! Below are some tips for staying 'green' *and* for saving money.

A solar-powered fence unit.

Electric lighting

First of all, switch lights off when not required! In small private yards it is easy to monitor lights being left on, but considerably more difficult in large, busy yards. Put up fierce notices underneath all light switches, demanding they be turned off after use. A draconian, though effective way of hammering home a directive is to threaten a 'fine' for every yard member should one person leave a light on. This generally a) makes the individual conscientious and aware of their actions or b) if they do genuinely forget to turn them off the fear of upsetting the entire yard leads to a confession. This same approach works with picking up droppings from the arena and other minor offences – it sounds terrible, but tried and tested, it works! Alternatively, install automatic timers. These do incur some expense but are definitely worth it, particularly for external lighting. Exterior sensor-operated lights are also good and can be programmed to stay on for as long or short a time as you need, before switching themselves off.

If possible, install low-energy light bulbs. There are several different options regarding low-energy bulbs, and it is an area of technology that is constantly being improved upon. Compact fluorescent light (CFL) bulbs are amongst the most common and one of the earliest low-energy bulbs to appear. They have come down in price since they were originally launched, and provide a good source of light. Light emitting diodes (LED lights) are a relatively recent low-energy form of lighting and are still being improved upon. They are very efficient, but can be quite expensive initially, and it is worth shopping around. Halogen bulbs are also more expensive to buy than the traditional bulb, but they should last on average for 2–5 years and use a fraction of the electricity.

Caution

Low-energy bulbs are not without their disadvantages, the most serious of which is related to CFL bulbs. These bulbs contain small amounts of the poisonous metal mercury. If a CFL bulb is accidentally smashed, mercury vapour, which is a health hazard, is emitted. In this situation, remove yourself and any animals from the area for 15 minutes. Then sweep up the broken bulb and place in a re-sealable sandwich bag or plastic bag and dispose of at a household hazardous waste unit (usually found at council recycling centres).

The risks of mercury poisoning are minimal provided you are sensible, and mercury poisoning is only a threat *if the bulb is broken*. LED lights do not contain mercury and there is a new generation of CFL bulbs called Alto bulbs which have a reduced mercury content.

Natural lighting

In order to increase natural lighting into stables, consider Perspex roofing panels. Obviously re-roofing is not something to be undertaken lightly, but if a situation arises whereby it needs to be done, then at that point consider your materials carefully. Provided roofs are maintained and kept relatively clean, then a single Perspex panel in a stable can allow in a considerable amount of light, particularly if combined with a sidewall window. The disadvantage with these panels (and with windows) is the lack of insulation and subsequent heat loss through the material; this needs to be offset against the light and ventilation they allow. In the UK in particular, where the winters are fairly temperate, this is less of an issue, and if necessary in extreme conditions a temporary insulating layer can be inserted (cardboard works well).

Indoor schools can really benefit from Perspex roof panels and also high side panels to allow in as much natural light as possible.

Insulation and ventilation

These two factors are related and so are considered together. Proper ventilation is extremely important in stabling, and the majority of stabling companies will automatically include this in their packages. Of greater

Perspex roof panels increase the benefits of natural lighting.

concern is the situation where very old stables are being used, or buildings that have been converted into stables, and in these instances the horse owner must ensure they provide sufficient ventilation. Generally, having an open top door in a stable (they should only ever be shut in extreme circumstances) and a vent in the back wall is sufficient, although a further front vent can be situated above the door frame. This will allow a drawing of air from front to back, thus helping the air to remain fresh. In barns and stable blocks, there should be covered roof vents, and sidewall vents, with the main doors being kept open when possible. It is important that there are 'inlets' and 'outlets' i.e., vents to allow the air in along the sidewalls or front of the stable/barn and vents to allow the air out, preferably in the roof – this allows for a circulation of air.

Roofs should ideally be insulated, particularly in steel barn constructions, which should also have a vapour barrier on the interior walls. This will prevent the build up of condensation when the warm air of the interior hits the colder surface of the metal walls. Tiled roofs have quite an insulating property owing to the nature of their fabric – much more so than, for example, a metal roof. Pole barns or wooden-built barns and stable blocks are generally 'warmer' than their metal counterpart. They can still be insulated although, in the UK, this is not so necessary.

Water supply

Water conservation is of primary concern in parts of the US and Australia for example, and has also become increasingly relevant in the UK.

One of the first steps is to fit hoses with turn-off valves at the end. This allows the water flow to be stopped during bathing, for example, immediately and conveniently. Better yet, bath the horse with a couple of buckets of water! Don't fill water troughs with a hose and then wander off leaving them to overflow.

Rainwater can be collected and utilised quite easily, and this is a practice that has become increasingly popular in the domestic forum as well. Currently rainwater can be used for flushing WCs, running washing machines, watering the garden, etc. For the equestrian environment collected rainwater can be used for drinking (provided the butts are kept spotlessly clean), for bathing, watering arenas, etc. If rainwater is to be collected, the roofing gutters must be kept absolutely clean (always a good idea anyway) and rain butts situated in appropriate locations. They must be on a hard, flat surface, and should be fitted with a lid to prevent accidents to children and animals, and also to prevent the butts becoming a breeding ground for insects – mosquitoes in particular.

One way of conserving water is to collect rainwater drained off from the roof by means of a small spout (see arrow).

Tip

A simple step towards saving water is placing water buckets in old tyres so they are not kicked over and spilt.

Always check the workings on field troughs and automatic water dispensers in stables to make sure they are not eroding. If the ball cock, for example, is punctured, the tank will continue to fill and overflow.

When situating troughs and tanks in fields, be very aware of where you place them. Don't put them under trees where leaves will fall in and pollute the water, try to locate them along a fence line that will allow one tank to serve two fields and don't put them right next to gateways, where the ground will quickly become poached. If running a yard, it is helpful to organise a rota where one person is allocated tank and fence duty for a period of time, and is responsible for checking both daily.

Also bear in mind the natural lie of the land and how water 'run off' from rain will occur in relation to muck piles and natural waterways – in other words make sure that your muck heap and barns are not draining down into and polluting a natural waterway.

Further suggestions about water management in pastures are given under the headings Pasture Management – Waterways later this chapter.

Sharing and scheduling

Sharing is a great way to cut down on costs and carbon footprints. Try to organise sharing, travelling and transport to shows amongst yard members and neighbours where possible. Also try sharing bulk or expensive products such as grooming products, feed supplements and (dependent on the yard situation) hay, bedding, etc. Sharing products can cause problems, but only if one person takes advantage. Try to set up sharing situations with good and trusted friends, and keep numbers low to avoid complications. Even horse sharing can be very successful given the right set of people, the right horse and the right circumstances. Sharing, or lending items of tack and horse clothing can also work, but always keep a careful record of any equipment that has been lent out, the date it went, and the person to whom it was loaned. Obviously, only share suitable items (for example, never swap equipment such as saddles and bits between horses unless they *definitely* fit correctly); always wash/clean thoroughly before swapping between horses (and never swap equipment that has been used on a horse with a contagious or infectious condition).

As a general principle, try to schedule visits from the farrier, equine dental technician and vet between several people to cut down on costs, time and carbon footprints. Clearly, particularly in the case of a veterinary emergency or urgent need of a farrier, this is not always practical, but it is good to keep it as a consideration. By the same token, if you are a single horse owner keeping a horse at home, and have to transport your horse to the farrier, then check with neighbours to see if you can set up a group of people in one location whose horses are on similar shoeing schedule, so you can travel together, thus saving fuel and money.

Also, try to regulate feed and bedding deliveries if individual yard members organise their own.

If trying to find somewhere to keep a horse, bear in mind the distance between the facility and your home. If there is somewhere within a cycling or walking distance, so much the better, *provided they also offer good amenities*.

Recycling

Try to recycle as much as possible.

- Set up recycling bins in the tack and feed rooms for cans, cardboard, paper, etc.

- All baling twine should be kept, preferably with the strings cut next to the knots.

- Keep feed bags; they can be used to store baling twine, for collecting floor sweepings and any number of other things. Some bags are recyclable: if you have too many of them, always check. Some of the more laminated bags are not recyclable but occasionally part of the bag might be. This does mean taking the outer cover and inner lining apart, but it is worth it. If you have safe and suitable facilities then burn bags rather than sending them to the landfill site.

- Supplement pots make really useful storage containers or measuring vessels. Always keep the lids and use them for storing any number of items. The larger containers can also be used for making dressage markers and even jump fillers for the more imaginative!

- Try to recycle all old pieces of equipment. Buckles (if not bent or otherwise damaged) can be removed from ancient headcollars or bridles and re-used, as can clips from broken lead ropes. Old cotton lead ropes that have worn or broken can be unravelled and the soft cotton pieces used when making your own fly fringe. Old rugs and blankets can be patched up and re-used, or relegated as dog beds. If unable to find a use for old equipment, and provided it is in safe repair, then consider donating it to charity.

'Green' ways of dealing with nuisances

Fly catchers

Flies are always a nuisance and can be really aggravating for a stabled horse. There are a number of fly spray dispensers available on the market formulated for equestrian barns and stable blocks, which dispense a regulated amount of fly spray at regular intervals. These can be helpful in combating the problem, but the majority of commercial fly sprays contain powerful man-made chemicals. An alternative is to use sticky fly strips hung high in the rafters, or to make your own fly traps, which again need to be strategically placed well out of reach of the horses. There are many different recipes for fly traps, some of which work on using really smelly bait (a distinct disadvantage in the barn) while others use sweet or sticky bait.

Vinegar mix
YOU WILL NEED

¼ pint (0.14 litre) vinegar
8 tbsp (120 g) sugar
A dash of water
Jam jar with lid, or paper and elastic band

STEP 1
Combine the vinegar and sugar in the jar and add enough water to make it about half full.

STEP 2
Put the lid on and punch holes in it, or cover the top with greaseproof paper (or Clingfilm), secure with an elastic band and punch holes in it.

STEP 3

Place out of reach of horses and children!

Sweet mix

YOU WILL NEED

A plastic drink bottle (1¾ pint/1 litre capacity, or thereabouts)
Fizzy drink, honey
Scissors
Duct tape

STEP 1

Take the bottle and cut it into two pieces approximately one-third of the way down.

STEP 2

Take the lid off. Fill the bottom piece of the bottle with 2–3 in (5–7.5 cm) of fizzy drink or honey, or any other suitable bait (this can be anything sweet or anything rancid and smelly).

STEP 3

Turn the top piece upside down and fit into the bottom piece, and tape the two pieces together. Simple, but effective – now hang it up high where it is out of reach.

The stages of making a sweet mix fly catcher.

Photos continue overleaf.

Making a sweet mix fly catcher.

For homemade fly spray recipes to apply straight to the horse see Chapter 5.

Minimsing rodent infestation

Cats

No equestrian facility is sacrosanct from rodents, no matter how clean and spotless – although the cleaner they are the more this does reduce infestations. The best way to combat the inevitable rodent problem (rats and mice) is a good farm cat, or preferably two. Finding the perfect cat is never easy, as many prefer to while away the days in front of a warm Aga, dining on store-bought delicacies. However, if the cat is encouraged to live around the stable yard and given a bed in the feed room or tack room, there is a possibility that it might live up to its reputation and spread fear amongst the rodent population. It is amazing what a deterrent a cat can be, and it is also a much 'greener' alternative to rodent problems than poison.

Barn owls

Barn owls are widespread across the world and are resident in parts of North America, Australia, much of Europe and parts of Africa and Asia. The barn owl population has decreased in many regions in recent years for a number of reasons including loss of habitat (barn conversions), and reduction in food caused by intensive farming practices. Consider erecting barn owl breeding boxes in suitable locations to encourage them to move in; not only

Caution

Always wear rubber gloves if handling a dead rodent.

are they magical birds to watch at dusk, but they are also great rodent killers. Generally they prefer a quiet location, but specifics on suitable boxes and placements for them can be found by contacting The Barn Owl Trust, www.thebarnowltrust.org.uk, or other barn owl sites found on the internet. (Barn owl numbers are also decreasing in the US and there are individual state-run organisations in operation to encourage numbers to increase – contacts can be found on the internet).

Goats: four-legged weed killers

Goats can be a really useful addition to a stable yard, and will happily eat weeds, shrubbery and tough grasses that are left untouched by horses. Goats can therefore be useful in keeping weeds under control around the stable yard, negating the need for chemical weed sprays, and can be 'spot' tethered to take care of a small area at a time.

Most horses will tolerate goats provided they are introduced slowly and carefully, and some come to actively enjoy their company. Introduce them through grazing in adjoining pastures first and, if necessary, then by penning the goats in small enclosures within the horse pasture.

Goats tend to be relatively low-maintenance, are generally hardier than sheep, and cause less impact to the ground than cows because of their small stature. They are, however, highly intelligent and can have a tendency to escape. Be warned against letting the goat have free range of the yard as they will eat everything including roses, flowers, blankets and anything else to hand. Also be aware that some goats have a predilection to nibbling horses' tails.

Hedgehogs: the bane of slugs

The hedgehog must be one of Britain's best-loved nocturnal creatures, helped along by Beatrix Potter's famous Mrs Tiggywinkle. Although the hedgehog is hardly an essential component of the stable yard, it is nonetheless lovely to encourage them to share the country lover's space. Their preferred habitat does overlap with that of the stable yard; they like hedgerows, long grasses and outbuildings and will often nest in hay barns. Be careful when cleaning out the barns and moving pallets under hay bales in case a hedgehog is hibernating or nesting underneath. If you wish to encourage hedgehogs to nest, try installing a hedgehog box in an outbuilding, but be prepared for a long wait – sometimes it takes up to a year for a hedgehog to move in. If possible, do not leave food out for them since you do not want

Barn owls

A study of barn owls published by the Connecticut Department of Environmental Protection's Wildlife Division demonstrates that a pair of barn owls with three young will kill over 1,000 rodents during an average three-month nesting period.

also to encourage rats and mice. (Incidentally, some of the food people have traditionally left out for hedgehogs – including cat food containing jelly, and bread and milk, is actually harmful to them.) Hedgehogs are inquisitive and will lick and smell new substances, so with this in mind try to avoid using any toxic chemicals such as slug or weed killers (the hedgehogs will kill your slugs anyway).

Increasing revenue

The potential to increase the revenue of the stable yard is very much dependent on the specific situation, location, facilities, etc., but there are generally many different ways in which to add a little extra income to the monthly earnings. Below are a few ideas that can help, some of which appear obvious, but often it is the most obvious that is overlooked!

- Consider renting out facilities such as indoor/outdoor schools, cross-country course and show jumps. These can be rented to individuals or to groups. It can be helpful to offer an incentive to the individual, e.g. six sessions for the price of five, or something similar.

- If opening a new yard or facility, contact all the local Riding Clubs and Pony Clubs to let them know what you have on offer (though word travels fast anyway in the equestrian community!).

- Organise training days, clinics and seminars, and try to attract the prestigious names in specific disciplines to raise awareness of the yard's reputation.

- The yard should always be kept spotless. However, on days when members of the public are coming in make sure that small details such as the state of the lavatories (don't run out of loo paper) have not been forgotten. It is worth delegating someone to be in charge of these types of things, and it can also be a nice touch to offer free cups of tea and coffee (dependent on numbers).

- Consider targeting other areas of speciality within the equestrian fold. For example, Western riding is an increasingly popular discipline and, by aligning a yard with both Western and English riding, you increase the size of a potential market. Other specialist areas to consider for hosting seminars and training days might be side-saddle, vaulting and driving, dependent on facilities.

- Natural horsemanship clinics also have a huge and increasing following, and if you are able to secure one of the leading names in this sector then running clinics or seminars is a good way of attracting people.

- When running training days and clinics, charge for non-riding participants as well as those bringing horses, though at a reduced rate.

- It can be worth approaching local schools to organise day trips out to teach young children basic horse sense and farm awareness.

- Utilise all buildings and outbuildings on the complex. Provided that buildings are weatherproof and secure they can be rented out as storage units for machinery, or as work shops. If you are willing to make a bigger investment then consider converting unused farm buildings into perhaps a tack shop or feed shop to be rented out or run by yourself, or as office units or other small business units. Obviously check thoroughly with the council about planning permission and the legal aspects to this type of conversion. It might also be useful to have a chat with your accountant regarding financial feasibility and tax implications. Although this involves an initial outlay, the return is generally good. Tack or feed shops are particularly relevant and beneficial to an equestrian location.

Essential

Be absolutely certain that you have adequate insurance cover.

Caution

If renting out units or buildings be aware of increased security risks with a larger passage of people passing through or by the yard.

Bedding and manure

Choosing bedding

There are a number of bedding options available, with new ones hitting the market virtually every day, and of these quite a few are marketed as eco-friendly. In particular there are companies that specialise in bedding products made from re-cycled cardboard and paper, which are biodegradable (in time) and easy to manage, although they can be expensive. Both these materials will decompose more quickly than wood chips or shavings.

An alternative to the traditional methods of bedding down a stable, either daily or deep littering, is to use thick rubber matting (there are ones made from recycled rubber) with just a small amount of bedding on top to absorb urine. This system can work well and cut down on waste and time, but it does depend on the horse. For horses that lie down a lot in the stable, the matting will not always provide sufficient cushioning, and it is possible for them to develop pressure sores. This can be rectified by using a thicker top layer of bedding.

It is possible to make your own paper bedding by shredding old paper

Tip

Try picking droppings out of the bedding using rubber gloves instead of a fork. This way just the dropping can be lifted without also removing excess bedding, which helps to keep the manure pile more manageable.

(you need an industrial-size shredder). If you spread the word, generally neighbours and friends will donate their old papers to you and it is possible to generate a fair amount of bedding. When doing this make sure that all metal staples, paper clips and any other potentially dangerous objects are removed from the paper. Also be aware that glossy papers are non-absorbent.

Paper and cardboard beddings are particularly good for horses with dust allergies because of their relatively dust-free nature, although alternative bedding such as hemp and flax is also manufactured as 'dust-extracted'. These materials are produced by a number of different companies and are eco-friendly in that they are organic products and biodegradable. Some companies market their products as made from fully sustainable and renewable sources without the addition of any chemicals.

Management and disposal of manure

Manure is one of the biggest problems with any equestrian facility – it is produced much more quickly than it rots down, and it can be a serious pollutant if it is not managed correctly.

With any yard environment, whether commercial or private, the location of the manure heap(s) should be a primary concern. Ideally, permanent heaps should be on an impermeable base such as concrete and be three-sided. The manure should be piled and managed to maintain a flat and condensed heap, which will increase the speed at which it rots. Heaps must be away from any natural watercourses and/or drainage ditches to prevent run-off polluting the water. Large commercial yards should, in principle, have their permanent heaps built on a slightly slanted surface that drains from the muck heap to an underground collection tank to prevent water run-off causing contamination. If an underground tank is not possible then the heap should drain to the back, not the front.

Non-permanent heaps in fields, etc. should, as a guide, be a minimum of 33 ft (10 m) from a watercourse, and at least 55 yards (50 m) from a spring, well or borehole.

Manure heaps should not be on, or close to, a property boundary and should be away from residences and from the stable block or barn. They should be easily accessible by tractor and wheelbarrow, and should be maintained daily to keep them neat and to aid decomposition.

It is ideal if the manure can be spread straight onto farmland, although with a reduction in the number of small farms this happens less often than formerly. Large commercial yards (generally) have to dispose of their manure through a licensed waste disposal contractor, and are subject to greater legislation than the private horse owner, although they are allowed to compost waste on their own land if they are able.

Composting is the most effective and eco-friendly method of waste management, and should be practised whenever possible. Heaps must be allowed to rot down for at least one year if they are to be spread back on horse pastures. This is to ensure that any fly eggs or larvae have died and to prevent the spreading of worms. For general garden composting the manure may be used more quickly, dependent on the speed of decomposition. Where possible (and most applicable to small yards), it is ideal to set up a system of three purpose-built, three-sided manure piles. The oldest bay will contain 'the compost' (the most decomposed pile), the middle bay, once filled, is allowed to decompose and the third bay is where fresh manure is piled. This system takes some time to set up, but once working is an efficient way to manage the manure.

Wherever possible, the speed of decomposition can be aided by continually turning over the heap. Composting and decomposition works by a mixture of heat, air and water. The matter in the middle will heat up quickly; by turning the pile, matter on the top surface is mixed in with that in the middle, which will allow air in to increase the rate of decomposition, and allow the pile to decompose more uniformly. If the pile is moist (not wet) this will help to prevent it overheating, as there is a risk of overheating (over 160°F/71°C), which will kill the useful microbes and organisms that aid decomposition and can lead to spontaneous combustion. Turning a small heap with a fork does not take too long, though is hard work, and large heaps can be turned with a tractor.

Muck piles from 'traditional' straw bedding were popular amongst mushroom farmers and for agricultural use, however straw as a bedding is being used less and less, and being replaced largely by wood chips, paper or hemp. These alternatives have positive aspects (as well as negative) with wood chips and shavings in particular taking longer to rot down, and so being less popular with farmers.

Manure can be bagged up and given away or sold. Alternatively, contact local garden centres and allotments to see if they would be interested in a steady supply of compost. It can also be worth contacting stately homes and country estates, country hotels and any other businesses that run large, landscaped gardens to see if they might also be interested in a supply of compost.

Pasture management

Good pasture management is the only way to ensure that you get the most from your fields, and with land at a premium there is no room for wastage. In the UK, as a guide, allow 1–2 acres (0.4–0.8 hectares) per horse, which should provide the space and fodder they need. Successful pasture management rests on rotation, so avoid over-grazing and set in place a system of resting pastures between use. Mixed grazing can also be beneficial (see Rotation below). Always pick up horse droppings from the pasture. If done on a daily basis this does not take too long; for larger yards dealing with many horses there are commercial muck sweepers available. Removing droppings will make a substantial difference to the worm burden of the field.

Good pasture management benefits the land, the horses and your long-term finances.

Rotation

Divide the land up into several fields. The actual number will be dependent on the total area involved, but a minimum of two, and preferably four. Where possible, designate winter pastures, which should have shelter, hardy grass, be well-draining and preferably nearer to the yard, and summer pastures, which must also provide shelter. Graze the horse(s) in one pasture for a period of 3–4 weeks at time, or dependent on the impact they have – i.e., the grass should not be grazed down below 2 in (5 cm). Then move them to the next pasture and, if possible, graze cattle or sheep on the first pasture for 2 weeks, before allowing it 4 weeks to recover. Cattle and sheep will eat grasses that horses will not, and cattle can help to keep the worm burden down – worms that affect the equine gut are killed in the bovine gut. This is also potentially a way to raise money, since it might be possible to rent out the grazing on a short-term (though regular) basis.

If it is not possible to mix-graze the pasture then keep the grass in resting pastures topped, which will help to keep weeds down and improve the overall quality of the grass. Resting fields can be lightly harrowed, if necessary. They should certainly be harrowed in the early spring to remove dead grass and aerate the soil, which encourages grass growth. Land that becomes uneven or poached (this should be avoided if possible) can be harrowed then rolled, then rested. This is best done in the early spring or the autumn. When rolling, the ground must be sufficiently wet to allow it to be flattened, but not too wet otherwise the tractor and roller will cause greater damage to the land. Rolling in the spring should be kept to a minimum where possible as it compresses the surface soil, which can discourage grass growth. In winter, summer pastures can be mix-grazed (cattle or sheep) for a time, before being allowed to rest and recover for the following spring. Conversely, in summer, keep winter pastures topped through mixed grazing for a time before allowing them to rest and recover for the winter grazing schedule.

Fertilising

Fertilising should only be carried out if the land warrants it (have a soil sample tested) and, if it does, then try to use an organic fertiliser such as farmyard manure, which is very good for alkaline soils, or lime for acidic soils. If the pasture does need to be fertilised then rest it afterwards to allow the fertiliser to wash into the ground. Ideally, a further soil sample should be tested to ascertain that the fertiliser has worked. If you know you have poor soil that does need routine fertilising then consider fertilising several times during the growing season, rather than once, as this promotes a more consistent level of nutrient in the soil. Harrow, roll and fertilise as necessary when a pasture is being rested.

Grasses, herbs and weeds

There are many, many different varieties of grass, some of which are better suited to some soils, climate and location than others. Horses are also picky eaters, and will only eat certain grasses with relish. If your pasture needs re-seeding (which is best done in autumn or early spring) then it pays to consult a seed merchant for advice on the best mix of grasses to use, dependent on your location, soil and requirements. Some good grasses are meadow grass, cocksfoot, timothy, perennial rye grass and the legume alfalfa. Once a pasture has been re-seeded or partially re-seeded allow it to rest and the grass time to take hold.

Herbs

Some wild herbs are really good for horses and they love them. Try to encourage wild herbs such as garlic, chamomile, wild thyme, marjoram, chicory, sheep's parsley, comfrey and yarrow, as well as white and red clover (in moderation) to grow. Herbs can either be planted along the edges of the fields, or included in a grass mix and used if re-seeding.

Weeds

In theory, if a pasture is well maintained then weeds will be minimal. Noxious weeds such as ragwort should be dug up and burnt immediately they are spotted. Other common weeds such as nettles, docks and thistles should also, ideally, be dug up or pulled. Regular mowing will stop these weeds from spreading. Spot applications of weed-killer can be made (using a back pack and protective clothing), but are really best avoided. Weed-killers are highly toxic and the animals will need to be kept off the pasture after applying them. Try the 'greener' approach to managing weeds by pulling, mowing and mix grazing (as mentioned earlier, goats in particular are good 'weed-killers').

Hedgerows

Hedgerows are really important habitats for many species of wildlife; insects including butterflies and moths, and birds, and have suffered over the last few decades primarily because of the increasing size of agricultural fields. Many hedgerows have been removed (the government even issued grants to do so), although there has more recently been a reversal of that policy. In 1992 funds were made available to reinstate hedgerows and since 1997 hedgerows have been protected in England and Wales in an effort to re-establish these important habitats. Hedgerows are recognised as a primary habitat for over forty-seven species of conservation concern in the UK, of which around 10 per cent are globally threatened.

Not only does a good hedge provide a haven for wildlife; it also makes an excellent wind barrier for horses. Horses can be hard on hedges, however, and in order to protect them and their wildlife it is advisable to fence inside the hedge leaving a gap of some 3–4 ft (1 metre plus) between the field margin and the hedge. In this way the horses will still benefit from the shelter and wind barrier provided by the hedge, and the hedge can continue to provide refuge for its many inhabitants.

Waterways

Ideally, horses should be fenced away from natural waterways for two reasons – their own safety and to avoid pollution.

Although natural waterways might seem an ideal (and very 'green') watering source for horses in the field, this is rarely the case in practice. Even if there are no concerns about the actual quality of the water, natural waterways can become treacherous, steep-sided, boggy, slippery and dangerous for horses, particularly when they are jostling in a small area. There is also a danger of sand colic caused through sand and grit ingested with water during the drinking.

Waterways can be polluted through equine faeces and urine, and horses can also damage the fragile bank area of waterways, trampling, or tearing up the vegetation, destroying the habitat for other wildlife, and creating mud and dirt which is transported into the water.

With this in mind, natural waterways should be fenced off from fields where possible, allowing a margin of at least 30 ft (9 m), which is referred to as a buffer zone.

Feeding

Economy with feeding should never be at the expense of quality; there are, however, ways to be economical when approaching feeding.

- Cut down on waste by placing feed buckets inside old car tyres to prevent the horse from kicking them over.

- If the horse is prone to removing its manger then tie the manger in place with baling twine and quick-release knots to allow you to remove it for cleaning.

- Never feed directly on the ground in the field. Tipping grain on the ground can result in substantial waste.

- If feeding grain in the field use either long troughs or buckets in tyres spaced well apart, and away from fence lines.

- Feed only as much hay as is eaten, especially in the field.

- Feed hay in the stable using small-hole haynets, which slow the consumption rate down, and prevent too much waste through hay mixing in with the bedding.

- If feeding hay in the stable from the floor then consider installing a Haybar, or keep the bedding swept well to one side to prevent hay being contaminated and wasted in the bed.

The feed room and storage

- It is important to maintain an organised, clean, vermin- and horse-proof feed room. The cleaner the feed room is kept the less likelihood there is of vermin infestation.

- Feedstuffs should be stored off the floor, and opened bags should be in vermin-roof bins (see Chapter 6 for ideas on storage).

- Label all storage containers clearly.

- Only buy in what will be used within a set time so there are not piles of feed sacks stacked in the feed room. They will go off, and can again be targeted by rodents. In situations where, by necessity, a large quantity of feed is ordered in at one time (large yards) then store the sacks on pallets and off the ground. For the smaller yard, try to organise a schedule of feed purchasing on a weekly or bi-monthly basis.

- There is quite a range in price on compound or sweet feed mixes. Always check the ingredient labels to work out how different brands of feed are differing (or the same) and then price-check.

- It can be cheaper to feed traditional feedstuffs such as oats, barley, horse and pony nuts, chaff, maize and bran than compound feeds. If feeding traditional feeds be very clear about your horse's nutritional requirements and make sure that your feeding plan is worked out correctly according to your horse's needs. Although compound feeds are generally more expensive, they can be easier to work with.

- When buying supplements do research on the internet or in different shops as prices will vary considerably. Also check the ingredients; occasionally less well-known brands will contain the same ingredients, and do the same job, but be a fraction of the price of well-known brands.

- Only feed supplements if your horse *really* does require them. Some of them can be extremely expensive, and many of them make wild claims ('will improve the top line'), which can only be attained through a balance of work and feed.

- Use recycled milk jugs or coffee cans as feed scoops – but always weigh your feed, never feed by 'the can'.

Carrots

It may sound odd, but why not grow your own? Carrots are easy to grow and can be grown on a piece of unused ground around the yard, provided it is not in the shade. First, dig the soil really well. Carrots like a sunny spot and a light, sandy soil free from stones and with a fine tilth; they prefer a soil that has not been fertilised with manure for about one year. If the soil appears poor after digging it through, then sprinkle a little organic fertiliser (blood, fish and bone contains the major nutrients required) on top. Then plant the seeds in shallow drills approximately 1 in (2.5 cm) deep. When the seeds start to grow, carefully thin them out so there is roughly 2–4 in (5–10 cm) between plants.

During their growing season carrots like to be watered regularly; you can also feed them with seaweed fertiliser at this point. If you plant seeds in mid-February they should be ready in June; March seeds will be ready in July and April seeds will be ready late in July/August. If planted before April, the seeds will need to be covered with a cloche to prevent them frosting. The only draw-back with home-grown carrots is they are so good you will want to eat them rather than donate them to the horses!

Buying and storing hay

- Be very particular about the quality of hay you buy. It is worth paying more for really good hay than paying less for poor-quality stuff that might be detrimental to the horse, and will also end up being wasted.

- The best way to buy hay is to see it growing in the field. This way you know whether the crop is clean and what types of grass(es) it consists of. This is not always possible though, so check hay thoroughly before buying. Check for quality of grasses, absence of weeds, dust, mould (and dead rodents!). If possible it is better to buy small bales. Medium-sized and large bales might be cheaper but it is impossible to tell the quality of the hay in the middle of the bale.

- Store hay off the ground on pallets and preferably under cover.

- Keep the floor of the hay barn swept to help cut down on dust.

- Feed floor sweepings to cattle if they are on hand, or bag up (use old feed bags) and give/sell to locals with chickens, rabbits or other small domestic animals who might need them for bedding.

Haylage

This is expensive but suits some horses very well, especially those with dust allergies. The biggest consideration with haylage is that the bags must not be punctured otherwise the haylage will quickly mould. Haylage will only last about seven days once the bag has been opened, and if the weather is very hot, slightly less than this. Bear this in mind when deciding whether to buy large or small bales. Only buy large bales (which do work out cheaper) if you will use the bale within the week.

Regarding big bales, generally avoid feeding *silage* to horses. As traditionally produced (primarily as feed for ruminants), it is too acidic, has a lower fibre content and higher protein content than haylage and can (though it does not always) contain harmful micro-organisms. Although some companies are now producing silage specifically for horses, it is best to check with your vet first if you are considering trying it.

CHAPTER 8

Converting buildings for stabling

It is possible to convert existing buildings such as barns, outbuildings, farm buildings or even garages into stables, provided they meet certain specific criteria based on the welfare of the horse. Converting an existing building can be a good option over erecting new stables, which can be expensive, but will be purpose-made for the job. With this in mind it is important to balance the cost of building new stables that will be tailor-made for their purpose, against the cost and work involved in converting buildings.

Permission

Building regulations, and planning regulations, which are entirely different, vary greatly in different countries, and before embarking on any potential building project you must seek advice and then permission from the necessary bodies. In the UK, building regulations, which basically dictate the specifications of a building, such as required insulation etc., are national. Planning regulations, which involve the change of use of a building, or the process required in order to erect a new building, are national, but there can also be some variance, especially in interpretation, between different local authorities. In the US always check with either the Zoning Division of the County Development Office, the Building Division of the County Development Office, or a similar governmental department to find out what permits or procedures are needed before considering a conversion (or a new-build). In the UK always check with the Local Planning Authority (LPA) to see if permission is required.

In the UK, permission is *normally* required to change the use of a build-

A horse at home in a converted building.

ing, e.g., to turn an agricultural barn into a horse barn with interior stabling (note that, in most contexts, UK legislation doesn't consider the horse an agricultural animal), and is *normally* required to erect new buildings.

Generally speaking, permission is more likely to be granted to convert an existing building than to erect a new building (this is particularly relevant in 'green belt' areas). Generally, planning departments are helpful and are a good source of free advice, so it is worth contacting the LPA for an informal chat before submitting any plans in order to get an idea of what restrictions you might be facing. (However, be aware that what you understood to be okay on the basis of the informal chat might be rejected later – so keep checking!) Planning rules will vary from one authority to another, and in some areas it is possible to erect a building such as a stable within the perimeter of your back garden without formal permission – though this is not always the best place to situate your stable(s). The LPA will assess the site and your proposal including its potential impact on the local environment, access to the site, and matters such as manure storage and disposal, and natural watercourses. It is essential to have thought of these issues before approaching the planners (whether going for a new-build or a conversion), and it is also a good idea to talk to your neighbours and get them on-side. It is advisable to always check first before building or making conversions/ alterations because if work is done without permission you might be ordered to take it down.

Location

- The location of your potential stable(s), whether being converted, or new-build, is a primary concern, and will be evaluated by the LPA and other relevant authorities if they are involved. If converting buildings, make sure that they are in a suitable and workable location for stables.

- They should have easy vehicular access, both to allow for transport of horses, vets, farriers and yard supplies, and also to facilitate delivery of building supplies.

- The buildings should be out of the prevailing winds, otherwise rain and snow will be driven in through the doorway and the stable(s) will be extremely cold.

- Generally, stables are best if they face eastwards. Obviously this is not always possible when converting buildings, but it is worth considering. East-facing stables will get the sun in the morning, but not become too hot in summer, and will face away from the prevailing westerly winds. (However, bear in mind the geography and climate of your locality: if you live on the east coast, easterly winds can be very chilly, especially in winter.)

- Water supply is a primary concern when considering stables. They need to be near a supply of fresh water, and in the UK will need fixtures/fittings that conform to the 1999 Water Fittings Regulations. These are in place for a number of reasons, one of which is to prevent water contamination through water being sucked back into the mains from dirty tanks/troughs, and for conservation matters. Measures required include fitting a stop valve and making sure the supply is insulated to prevent freezing in winter, amongst others things (check with Defra for further information: www.defra.gov.uk). Some plumbing work, such as plumbing-in automatic waterers, might require permission from the water company so check with them first before you do anything. Obviously taps and fixtures/fittings (other than waterers) must be outside the stable/s and safe from equine intervention.

- A further water consideration is the lie of the land and the natural watercourses surrounding the stable conversion (or new-build). The building should not be adjacent to, or near, any natural watercourse since there is a very real danger of water contamination through run-off from stable buildings and manure piles.

- Related to this is drainage (see Floors later this chapter). The stable should be set up to drain into specific drains preferably at the front, or else the back of the building. Location of the manure pile should be similarly considered (see Chapter 7).

- A power supply is not *essential* for a stable, but is certainly preferable if possible. For example, consider lights for those dark evenings and any times when you might be going off to a show before the crack of dawn. Consider how far the stable site is from a power supply, or better yet, consider installing a solar panel system to power the stable. Although these can be expensive, if the building is some distance from the power supply cables then balance the cost of directing power cables to the site against the cost of solar panels. All cables and switches must be out of reach of the horses and safely secured within the building.

- In various respects, the site of the stable(s) should be convenient. In addition to the access considerations mentioned earlier, this means it should be either near to, or convenient for, the house, and within easy reach of the pasture (particularly your winter pastures so that turning out and bringing in is not too difficult during the short days).

- Also make sure that the building is near to (or incorporates) facilities such as feed room, tack room and hay store.

- Ideally there should be an area fenced off around the stable(s). This is to contain horses should they escape from the stable – or, if the stable is actually within the pasture perimeter, to keep horses that are turned out away from interfering with the stable environment.

Notes on types of building

Only buildings that meet certain criteria should be considered for conversion to stables. This is generally based on good common 'horse-sense', but further guidelines can be found in the Equine Industry Welfare Guidelines Compendium (available as a download on www.newc.co.uk), under Housing.

Only buildings that meet certain criteria will make successful conversions.

A first consideration is the size of the building and whether it is adequate for the horse. A stable should always be just a little too big, rather than too small, and must provide enough room for the horse to stand up, turn around and lie down with ease.

It is always better to think bigger; i.e. don't spend money on converting buildings into pony stables if in a few years they will be needed to house horses.

The building must provide enough headroom, which needs to be at least 3 ft (91 cm) clearance above the horse's head when standing. This means that the ceiling height needs to be between 9–12 ft (2.7–3.7 m) dependent on the size of horse/pony being housed.

Stable size guidelines

Pony stabling 12 x 12 ft (3.7 x 3.7 m)
Horse up to 16 hh 12 x 14 ft (3.7 x 4.3 m)
Horse over 16 hh 14 x 14 ft (4.3 x 4.3 m)
Foaling box 16 x 16 ft (4. x 4.8 m)

The doorway should also be sufficiently wide and high to allow safe passage and should always be split, with the top half kept pinned back, and doors must open outwards, never inwards. The exception to this is sliding doors, which can be useful if room is an issue. These should be purpose-built to allow the horse to see out and/or put its head out.

Door dimensions

Door width 4 ft (1.2 m)
Height of doorframe 8 ft (2.4 m)
Height of bottom half of door 4½ ft (1.4 m)
Height of top half of door 3½ ft (1.07 m)

NB: The height of the bottom half of the door can be altered according to the size of the horse.

Barns and cowsheds

Old barns or cowsheds can make useful conversions (you will need to check about 'change of use' planning permission), and can house a number of boxes, dependent on the size of the barn. This arrangement of internal stabling is extremely popular in the US (where the buildings are referred to as 'barns') and is becoming more so in the UK. The advantages of this type of stabling are many, with the major disadvantage being the ease with which diseases and vices can be transferred amongst the residents.

Generally when dividing up the interior of a barn to make stables it is easiest, and often cheaper, to buy ready-made partitioning panels that can then be assembled to the required size. There are a number of companies who specialise in these partitions, most of which are based on a steel frame construction with wooden tongue and groove panels on the lower half and a metal grille on the top half (although this will vary with design). Alternatively, partitions can be made from plywood – ¾ in (2 cm) being a minimum thickness to use), or from spaced boards with a maximum gap of 1½ in (3.8 cm) between. Spaced boards allow a good airflow through the boxes and easy communication between adjacent horses. If building a partition in this way, then it is necessary to use a central vertical support in the middle of the panel to strengthen the boards against a kick (see diagram). Another option is to build brick or breeze block (cinder block US) partitions; again it is worth price-checking the respective costs of this and the cost of purchasing ready-made panels. Any dividing partition must be at least 8 ft (2.4 m) high.

Partitions must also be flush with the floor to prevent any chance of the horse catching a foot underneath, and must, as mentioned, be a minimum of 8 ft (2.4 m) high, which is high enough to prevent the horse kicking out and catching a leg over the top.

Partitions do not need to be solid all the way up, but should be solid to a minimum of 4 ft (1.2 m) from the ground (this area is referred to as the kicking boards). The top of the panel can be a metal grille design, with bars of ¾–1 in (2–2.5 cm) thickness, spaced no more than 3 in (7.5 cm) apart. This design allows good airflow and communication between stablemates, but is not suitable for every horse (some horses are bullies and will snatch at their neighbours through the bars, which can be disturbing to the other horse).

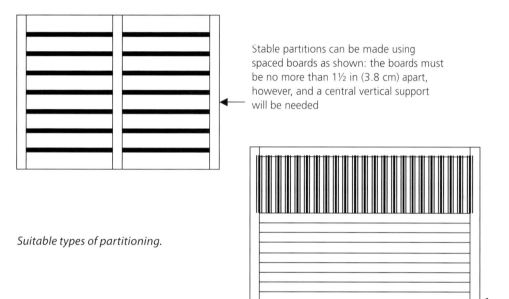

Stable partitions can be made using spaced boards as shown: the boards must be no more than 1½ in (3.8 cm) apart, however, and a central vertical support will be needed

Suitable types of partitioning.

Partitions made from tongue and groove boards on the lower half and spaced metal grille on the top half can be very good and allow plenty of ventilation and communication between horses: this design does not require a central vertical support

Garages

Garages can be converted into stables provided they can safely accommodate the horse. The advantage of converting a garage to a stable is that they usually have power to the building. (If power does run to the building, it is essential that that all cables and switches are covered and made safe.) Common disadvantages are lack of ceiling height and low rafters and, if this is the case, then the building should not be used (unless the issue is addressed, but this would normally result in major structural work). Dependent on the size and type of garage, either the entire building can be converted to a stable, in which case the up-and-over door will need to be removed and the front wall rebuilt with a suitable equine door installed (and possibly a further window) or, if the garage is very large, then the stable(s) can be partitioned on the inside using either purpose-built partitions or brick or breeze blocks (cinder block US).

If the garage has a regular walk-through door (as well as the up-and-over door) the handles/knobs, which the horse might injure itself on – or even open, will need to be removed and replaced with a flat sliding bolt or suitable equine lock. If the door opens inwards it will need to be removed and re-hung to open outwards.

Structural soundness

Any building being considered for conversion to stabling must obviously be totally structurally sound, and must be assessed for its viability. The walls need to be robust; brick, concrete, sound wood or steel. Tin is not a suitable wall fabric for stabling, and should be avoided as a roofing material, as should galvanised and corrugated iron sheeting. Dependent on the structure of the walls, it can be a good idea to add wooden kicking boards, or rubber matting to a height of 4 ft (1.2 m) around the interior of the stable. These provide some protection to both the wall and the horse if the horse kicks out, and rubber matting has the further benefit of providing some protection to the horse should it become cast.

Flooring

Sadly there is no *ideal* flooring for horses and every flooring system has its advantages and disadvantages. Flooring falls into two main categories, porous, which are basically sand and soil (gravel, despite being abrasive, is also used in the US), and non-porous, such as concrete or tarmac.

Porous floors

Floors such as sand or clay are primarily topsoil, and are good for the horse in that they are 'warm' floors and they have 'give', making them better for horses that spend a lot of time standing in the stable (never a good thing unless for veterinary reasons). However, they can be difficult to manage: they can hold the urine, are hard to clean out, hard to disinfect, can become slippery, can retain odour and can freeze. They need to be carefully maintained, topped up and levelled. Furthermore sand has the added disadvantage of mixing with the bedding, with the consequent possibility of being ingested, which can lead to sand colic.

If you need to work with an existing porous floor then it is a good idea to use thick, recycled rubber matting in conjunction with it. This matting can come either as solid sheets (very good also for use on non-porous concrete floors) or as grids. The grid type work well with a porous floor as they allow urine to drain through and away, without the ground becoming cut up by the horse. Rubber matting is expensive – there really is no way round this – but it is incredibly durable and should be a single one-off expense. Rubber mats also significantly reduce the amount of bedding required and in this respect will save money in the long term.

Non-porous floors

These are primarily concrete and tarmac. Concrete is one of the most widely used and popular floors (brushed or lightly ridged concrete should be used as it provides traction), owing primarily to the ease with which it can be maintained and cleaned. It is, however, very hard on the horse's legs, unforgiving and a 'cold' surface.

Concrete is expensive to put down, but again should be a one-off expense.

Most important with a non-porous floor is the drainage, and it is here that problems can occur when converting buildings into stables. Ideally (certainly if you were building stables from scratch), a concrete floor should be sloped slightly to allow urine, etc. to move towards a drainage channel at the front of the stable. Front drains are easier to keep clean and to monitor than drains at the back or middle of the floor. However, garages and other outbuildings will not generally have a floor designed to drain fluids, and the expense incurred in creating a new floor is not generally worth it, unless the floor needs re-laying for other reasons as well. Floors without drainage can be managed with careful mucking out and, provided you are vigilant about keeping the stable clean and the bedding swept up daily to allow the floor to dry off, they are workable.

If converting a building that does already have a drain in the floor, make sure it is absolutely safe for horses and is covered with something substantial enough to take the weight of the horse.

Tarmac is a slightly more forgiving surface than concrete and tends to be slightly 'warmer' too, but is not used as frequently.

Roofs

Roofs must be sound and weatherproof. Generally, flat-roofed buildings are not ideal, primarily because the roof is often too low, and unless they are well structured there is a tendency for water to pool. Roofs must be fire-retardant (which is pretty standard in roofing materials nowadays), preferably insulated and preferably 'quiet'. Suitable materials include tiles, shingles, board and felt, board and felt tiles. Tin roofs or galvanised iron sheeting should be avoided because of their noise level during rain, and lack of insulation.

Tip

Onduline roofing sheets are manufactured from 48% recycled material.

If it is necessary to re-roof the existing building try to opt for Onduline corrugated roofing sheets (in the US a similar product is called Ondura). This is a lightweight roofing material made from bitumen-saturated organic fibres. It is easy to work with, and is virtually maintenance-free. It is relatively expensive, but because of its lack of maintenance, pays off in the long run. It is available in several different colours and also in transparent sheets. It is a good idea, if possible, to include one or two transparent sheets per stable roof because they make a significant amount of difference to the amount of light in the stable. This roofing material will not rot or rust and generally comes with a 15-year guarantee.

All roofs should be fitted with gutters, preferably draining into water butts, which can then be used to water the garden, arenas, etc.

Condensation and insulation

Condensation can be a problem, particularly in metal barn/stable buildings with metal roofs. It occurs when moisture is formed from air as it cools when coming into contact with a cold surface. Insulation in the roof keeps the potentially cold interior roof surface nearer to the interior air temperature, and so reduces the chance of condensation. Some roofing materials such as Onduline, board and felt, and shingles have a degree of insulating property that will help to offset condensation in a temperate climate. In more extreme climates it will be necessary to provide a further layer of insulation.

Lighting and ventilation

Lighting

Light is an important factor in stabling. Transparent roofing panels, as mentioned, make a big difference. Windows, which aid ventilation, also help. If possible it is useful to have artificial lighting too. If lights are already in place then work with what you have. However, they must be out of reach of the horse and should ideally be towards the front or sides of the stable. Lights should be fitted with wire mesh or plastic covers to prevent danger of breakage, and all electrical cabling must be housed in metal or plastic conduit to protect it from rodents, and from the horse. Light switches should be on the exterior of the stable and should be specific exterior switches, i.e. waterproof. Use low-energy bulbs and consider solar panels as your power source, or solar-powered light kits.

If using a converted building, bear in mind that windows must be horse-friendly. This means that the horse must not be able to access the glass, or get trapped or caught on any part of the window or opening. Cover windows on the inside with a sheet of strong wire mesh. If you are able to do so, and if the glass is in poor condition, remove the window frame from the structure, remove the glass and replace with strong Perspex (still use mesh to keep the horse away from the window). Ideally the window should hinge at the bottom and swing outwards at the top (see diagram).

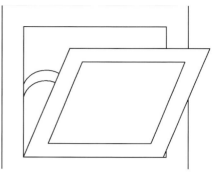

A suitable window for a stable.

Ventilation

Ventilation is absolutely essential in any stable environment, and, apart from aiding the horse, good ventilation will help to reduce condensation. Ventilation works in two ways: it should first incorporate an exchange of fresh air for stagnant air, and second should allow air to circulate throughout the stable (or barn). This means that there should be 'inflow' and 'outflow' – i.e. more than one opening which will allow air to come in and pass through the area. In custom-built stables or barns, ventilation vents come as standard, but when converting buildings into stables it is a factor that has to be considered. The most effective form of ventilation incorporates under-eave vents, (often called soffit vents) with ridge vents, which are located along the ridge of the roof. This system ensures a steady flow of fresh air into and around the stable environment.

Increasingly, modern buildings are fitted with both soffit and ridge vents, so it might be that your building for conversion already has some form of ventilation. Check this, and also make sure it is sufficient; a horse in a stable requires a much greater level of air circulation and fresh air than a car in a garage. Also, soffit vents fitted in residential-type buildings will often be covered with a fine mesh to prevent insects and dirt entering the building. These are not suitable for equestrian buildings as they do not allow enough air through. An open vent with no covering or a mesh of not less than one inch (2.5 cm) squares (to prevent birds flying in) should be used.

Older buildings might well not have any form of ventilation, and if this is the case it will be necessary to install some. Under-eave vents are relatively easy to install yourself if the building is timber-framed, although ridge vents are more complicated and not for the novice DIY person!

For a building being converted into a one-horse stable, i.e. a space of approximately 12 x 12 ft (3.7 x 3.7 m) or 12 x 14 ft (3.7 x 4.3 m), it is possible to get by without a ridge vent, but under-eave or wall vents must be added to the back wall of the building. This will allow air to enter through the front over the stable door and pass through to the back of the stable. If you decide to create a back window space to allow the horse to look out, and to increase air flow, make sure that it is not directly opposite the front door as this will create a draught rather than circulating air. Windows such as this are really useful and do provide the horse with an added level of interest, however they need to be fitted with a door on the outside that can be closed in bad weather. You will still need a back wall vent to ensure that air circulates when the back window is closed off.

Diagram showing air flowing through soffit vents under the eaves and out of ridge vents located along the spine of the roof.

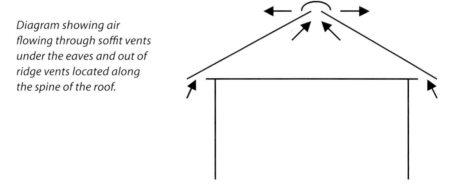

Barns that are being converted to house several horses must have eave and ridge vents. It is highly preferable for barns to have doorways at each end, and these should be kept open when possible to allow air through. However, these cannot be the only source of ventilation otherwise, when they are closed at night or in very poor weather, there will be no ventilation at all. Ideally, barns should incorporate either doors or windows on the exterior walls of the stables, which will again aid ventilation, although this is not always possible with conversions. In all cases, under-eave vents must be installed along the lengths of the building, with some form of ridge or roof vent added.

Stable fixtures and fittings

All fixtures and fittings in the stable must be smooth and safe for horses. Lights and power cables have already been discussed; further fixtures and fittings will include door bolts, window fastenings, water and feed facilities, tie-up rings and possibly stable 'entertainment' such as mirrors or toys. Bolts and latches for doors should be purpose-made equine ones, and should include a top bolt and a bottom kick bolt on standard opening and closing doors. Sliding doors come with their own inbuilt locking mechanisms. Bolts and latches will vary slightly in design and in cost. Research on the internet and price-check, but don't forget to factor in postage and packaging costs. Some horses are particularly adept at opening stable doors (hence the need for a bottom kick bolt!), if this is the case then try using an old lead rope clip through the bolt as a further locking device. (With a true escape artist, it might even be necessary to fit a second sliding bolt near the bottom of the door, and secure this one with a clip!)

The horse should not be able to access the window or its fastenings as these should be secured behind a metal grille for safety. When choosing fastenings opt for simple and easy patterns, and consider ones that are operable while wearing thick winter gloves!

Keep the area for watering in the stable separate from the area where the horse will be fed, otherwise horses have a tendency to drop their feed in their water. Automatic waterers have their advantages, but are expensive to install. Their main advantage is they negate having to trudge with heavy buckets, and they can be heated – which is useful in extreme climates – but they do need to be maintained and cleaned as regularly as a bucket, and if you use waterers they should be fitted with a drinking gauge to allow you to monitor the amount the horse is drinking.

Water buckets can be hung from the wall or placed on the ground, depending on personal preference, and the temperament of the horse. It is better for the horse to drink from the ground since this is the most natural position. However, if a horse is prone to kicking its buckets around, then hang them from the wall. The best fittings to do this are clips attached to metal plates, which can be screwed into the wall joists. The bucket handle then clips on and is hung. These are safe with or without the bucket attached. The clip should be positioned so that the bucket rim hangs just above the level of the horse's chest, and is best positioned on the inside of the front wall on one side of the door, for easy access and monitoring. Alternatively, place buckets on the floor in one of the front corners. For extra stability try placing the bucket inside an old car tyre.

As with drinking, it is preferable for the horse to eat from the ground. Feed on the opposite side of the stable from the water station, and again use an old car tyre to secure the bucket and prevent it being kicked around. Alternatively, you can hang a bucket in a similar fashion to the water bucket. If you prefer to use a corner manger then position it at a similar height, and in a front corner. Many horses become agitated when eating and if the manager is in the back corner of the stable they rush between a mouthful of food and hanging their heads over the door. Mangers placed at the front of the stable ease this anxiety. Only install managers that can be removed to be cleaned.

Hay, also, should ideally be fed from ground level, although this does not work in every case. The disadvantage of feeding hay from the ground is the potential for it to become soiled and mixed in with the bedding. This problem can be solved by installing a ground-level hay manger, with one of the best such products being the Haybar. Avoid at all costs the traditional wooden slatted, or metal hay manger positioned on the wall; there is a danger with these of dust and hay particles falling in the horse's eyes, and the structure itself poses a threat if the horse kicks out or rears.

If haynets are to be used then position the tie-up ring high on the wall, and away from the water station. The bottom of the haynet should not be lower than the horse's withers. Haynets with small holes are safer to use as there is less possibility of the horse actually catching a foot in them.

It is useful to have several tie-up rings in the stable, one on either side for cross-tying and one at the back in case it is necessary to tie the horse up out of the way while working at the front of the stable. Use purpose-built rings attached to a metal plate that can be screwed into the wall, and position them at withers height or above. Attachments of this sort are generally available from any hardware store, and most equestrian retailers, as well as on the internet.

Fire precautions

A fire in the stable/barn/yard is the most devastating and horrific thing to happen, and in many cases is avoidable. The speed with which a fire will move through a stable block or barn is terrifyingly, and in the case of such an event every person must act with immediacy and assurance in order to minimise damage. Basically the stable environment is a fire waiting to happen; it is full of dry combustible components, much more so than the average home, and every precaution must be taken to minimise the risk of fire.

There must be the correct type of fire extinguishers clearly accessible, and in prominent view outside the front of the stables, and you must understand how to use them – in the case of an emergency there is no time to be reading instructions or trying to figure things out. In yards there should be a clearly displayed fire drill and evacuation process in the event of a fire, which every-one should be familiar with. It is wise to occasionally practise the evacuation

Essential

Install smoke alarms and/or heat detectors in stables and barns.

procedure, and fire extinguishers should be regularly tested and serviced to make sure they work.

Fire safety measures

- One of the leading causes of fires is electrical, so if you are converting an existing old building into a stable make sure the electrical systems are sound, serviceable and suitable for 'agricultural' use. Make regular checks of cables for rodent damage, keep light fittings free of cobwebs and dust, and unplug all electrical appliances such as clippers, kettles and radios at the end of the day.

- Never store hay above the stables. This is a tradition that was popular in old American-style barns and is still practised in some areas. This is a major fire hazard and should never be done. Hay and bedding storage should be situated away from the stables or barn.

- Monitor hay bales – if baled wet they can ferment and rapidly heat up and combust (and such hay should not be fed anyway!). Similarly, monitor the muck heaps, which can also reach combustible temperatures in the middle.

- Always situate muck heaps away from the stables or barn.

- Keep the barn, stables and hay/feed/bedding areas clean, swept up and free of cobwebs.

- Enforce a **NO SMOKING** policy on the yard.

- Make sure that headcollars and lead ropes hang outside every stable at all times, so a horse can be evacuated under control if necessary.

- Make sure that vehicle access to the stable or barn is always kept clear and functional in case emergency vehicles need to get in.

- Practise good stable management to minimise the risk of a fire starting.

Warning

Straw will reach a burning temperature of approximately 300ºF (149ºC) within 2–5 minutes. If a horse is to survive a stable fire unharmed it must be evacuated within **30 SECONDS**.

CHAPTER 9

Jumps and dressage arenas

Show jumps

Building show jumps from scratch is not particularly easy unless you are a capable woodworker. It can be time-consuming and also – if buying the raw materials – quite expensive (wood is by no means cheap). However, once you have made one set, and are comfortable with the tools and processes, it can be great fun to create your own jumps. In this chapter are instructions for two basic types of wing; this provides a springboard from which you can leap into more complicated structures. An in-depth discussion about building show jumps is grounds for a book in itself, and there is a good book on the market, Andy Radford's *Building Show Jumps*, which covers different types of jump in greater detail than space allows for here.

As always, try to balance the time and cost of building your own with the expense of buying jumps. There are many companies specialising in jumps at the moment and there is, in general, a fairly substantial range of prices. Jumps made from plastic polymer offer an alternative to traditional wooden jumps. They do not rot and are easy to handle, these again range in price and are definitely worth checking around. Another good place to look for jumps is eBay: often there are pretty good deals on sets of wings and poles, provided you can pick them up! Alternatively try contacting local Riding or Pony Clubs to see if they might be selling off any of their old jumps. Purchasing old second-hand jumps, and spending a little time on doing them up, can be a really cost-effective way of getting started on collecting a set of jumps. Sometimes they need nothing more than a good sanding and re-painting, and often if sections of them have rotted they can be repaired and replaced.

Making feet and wings

Although it is not essential, it is preferable to make (or buy) jumps that have detachable feet. This is for safety reasons, to decrease the chance of a wing shattering when hit, and also makes the jumps much easier to store.

Safety first

Always use common sense when using tools.

Only use tools you are familiar and comfortable with.

Never work with power tools near horses; try to limit work to a tool shed or workshop.

Whenever you are using power tools always use a circuit breaker.

Whenever you are sanding or cutting wood always wear goggles to prevent dust/splinters getting in your eyes.

Always check the cables and plugs of power tools to make sure they are in good working order.

Do not use power tools in the wet, or damp conditions.

Never leave tools or nails, etc. lying around, and especially not in any area where the horse might have access.

Standard jump feet

When setting about building your own jump wings start by making the feet.

TOOLS YOU WILL NEED

Workbench with clamps

Saw

Hacksaw (if cutting threaded rod)

Sander

Metal ruler or tri-square

Drill and drill bits

Rubber mallet

Spanner (wrench US)

Tape measure

Pencil

Chisel (1 in/2.5 cm minimum)

MATERIALS YOU WILL NEED

Two 2 ft x 6 in x 2 in (61 x 15 x 5 cm) wooden planks

Two metal back plates

One 39 in (1 m) length threaded rod (1 in/25 mm diameter works well), or 4 in
   (10 cm) bolts of the same diameter

Eight washers and nuts (or wing nuts) to fit the threaded rod

STEP **1**

First trim the top two corners of both pieces of wood. This is a safety measure so there are no sharp areas on the foot in case of an accident, and it also improves the look. Lay the two pieces of wood on a flat work surface or preferably a workbench where they can be clamped, with the 6 in (15 cm) surface facing upwards. At each end of each piece measure 2 in (5 cm) down towards the bottom and make a pencil mark. Next, measure 6 in (15 cm) along the top towards the middle of the length on each end, and make a pencil mark. Take a ruler and connect the two marks. You should now have a triangle marked out in the top two corners. Carefully saw these off and then sand the edges well – remember this edge is the top edge of the foot.

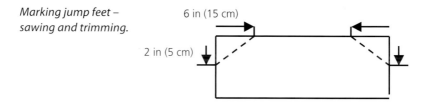

Marking jump feet – sawing and trimming.

6 in (15 cm)

2 in (5 cm)

STEP **2**

The next stage is to cut a channel in each foot into which the jump wing upright can slot – this is called a 'halving joint' and needs to be in the centre of the foot. Place the tape measure along the length of wood and make a mark in the middle, which should be 12 in (30 cm): using the tri-square draw a straight vertical line down the 6 in (15 cm) face of the wood. Now measure 1 in (2.5 cm) on either side of the line and draw two more lines. These mark the width of the channel that needs to be cut. Next turn the wood so the 2 in (5 cm) side is facing upwards and continue the channel lines on this side to a depth of ½ in (1.25 cm). Do this on the top and bottom of the 2 in (5 cm) sides of the wood.

Now you need to cut out the channel carefully! Take a saw and cut down through the three pencil lines you have drawn, to the depth indicated on the top, i.e. 0.5 in (1.25 cm). Sawing through the middle line as well as the outside edges makes removing the wood in the channel easier. Once you have made

Tip

If anything, the channel should be slightly on the small side so that the wing upright has a really solid, tight fit. With this in mind, saw to the inside of your guideline, not the outside.

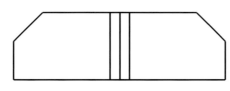

Making jump feet – creating the channel.

your cuts, take a chisel and remove the pieces of wood, then sand down so the edges are smooth. You should now have two pieces of wood with sloping topside corners and a ½ in (1.25 cm) channel running vertically down the middle of their length.

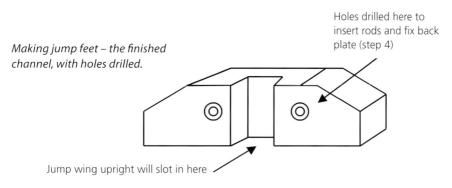

Holes drilled here to insert rods and fix back plate (step 4)

Making jump feet – the finished channel, with holes drilled.

Jump wing upright will slot in here

STEP 3

The bottom of the jump wing uprights (to make these, see next section – Basic Jump Wing) must now be cut away so that they slot into the channels created in the feet; this constitutes the second half of the 'halving joint'. Place the jump wing upright on the workbench with the 2 in (5 cm) side facing upwards and measure 6 in (15 cm) from the bottom of the piece. This is the height of the foot. Draw a pencil line at 6 in (15 cm) horizontally across the 2 in (5 cm) face. Next, turn the wood over so that the 4 in (10 cm) side is facing upwards and measure 1 in (1.25 cm) inwards (still at the 6 in/15 cm height). Draw this, then draw a vertical line to the bottom of the wood to provide the saw guide line. Do this on both 4 in (10 cm) faces. You should now have a 6 in (15 cm) high and 1 in (1.25 cm) deep area marked out. Turn the wood back so that the 2 in (5 cm) side is facing upwards and carefully saw through the drawn lines. You should now have a chunk cut away from the jump upright, which will slot into the foot.

6 in (15 cm)

1 in (2.5 cm)

Making jump feet – trimming the upright.

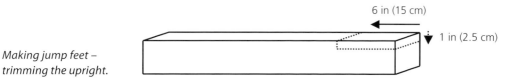

STEP 4

Each foot section now needs to be drilled to accommodate the threaded rod and metal plate, which will keep the jump wing upright and foot bolted together. Place the pre-drilled back plate centrally over the channel on the foot and mark the centre of the two holes with a pencil. Using an appropriate sized drill bit, drill the two holes. Insert the jump wing upright in the foot channel, allowing the lip of the wing to sit on the top of the foot; this keeps it secure and prevents it slipping. Use a rubber mallet if necessary to get the wing upright into the channel. Push the threaded rod or bolt through the front of the foot, and slide the back plate on to secure the upright. Then screw the washers and nuts onto the rod, holding the back plate in place. Use a spanner to get a really good, solid and tight fit. (If you use wing nuts rather than standard nuts, this can make assembling and dismantling easier.)

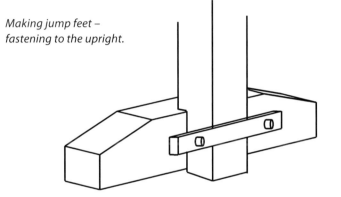

Making jump feet – fastening to the upright.

Basic jump wings

These instructions are geared towards making a 4 ft (1.2 m) high set of wings. You will already have made the feet as outlined above.

TOOLS YOU WILL NEED

Workbench with clamps
Saw
Sander
Metal ruler or tri-square
Drill and drill bits
Rubber mallet
Spanner (wrench US)
Tape measure
Pencil

MATERIALS YOU WILL NEED

(NOT INCLUDING THOSE FOR THE FEET, SEE ABOVE)

Three wooden rails 10 ft x 4 in x 2 in (3 m x 10 cm x 5 cm) to make the jump
   uprights, front and back

Three wooden planks 12 ft x 3 in x 1 in (3.7 m x 7.5 cm x 2.5 cm) to make the
   jump's frame

Appropriate bolts, nuts and washers

Sixteen 1½ in (38 mm) screws

STEP 1

First take the 10 ft x 4 in (3 m x 10 cm) rail and cut into two 4 ft (1.2 m)
lengths; these will form the front upright of each jump wing, where the jump
cups will sit. Put these on one side and, still working with the 10 ft x 4 in
(3 m x 10 cm) wood, now cut two 2½ ft (76 cm) lengths – these will form the
back, shorter uprights of the jump wings. Next, take the 12 ft x 3 in (3.6 m x
7.5 cm) rail and cut it into two 3 ft (91 cm) lengths; these will form the
bottom horizontal supports of the jump wings.

STEP 2

At this point, if you have not already done so, then cut the halving joints on
the jump wing uprights (the 4 ft/1.2 m and 2½ ft/76 cm lengths), as described
in the sequence above for making standard jump feet. Next, and working on
one wing at a time, lay a 4 ft (1.2 m) and a 2½ ft (76 cm) section on the
ground parallel to each other, making sure the 'foot' end is pointing down
on both pieces. From the bottom of the foot end measure 6½ in (16.5 cm)
up and make a mark. This mark should now be ½ in (1.25 cm) above the
channelled-out piece that will take the foot. Make sure the level is the same
on both the long and short uprights, then lay the 3 ft (91 cm) plank with its
bottom edge along the marked line. Temporarily secure in place with a screw.
(Be careful not to split the wood, pre-drill your hole if necessary). Now
measure the distance between the top of the uprights and make sure it is the
same as at the bottom – they must be absolutely parallel to each other.

STEP 3

Now place the remaining 6 ft (1.83 m) length of the 3 in (7.5 cm) rail diagonally across the top of the jump uprights. Allow the rail to overhang at either
side and again check that the uprights are parallel. Taking a pencil, mark the
excess of the wood that needs to be cut from each end of the rail, then carefully saw off. The rail should now line up exactly with the uprights. Temporarily secure in place with a single screw to each side.

STEP 4

The wing now needs to be bolted together. Check one last time that the uprights are parallel! Then drill a hole in the centre of each corner. Once the holes have been made you can drive the bolts through (you might need the rubber mallet), turn the wing over, place washers over the bolt and then tighten the nuts.

STEP 5

The basic frame is now complete. It is now time to make the jump cup holes and to add the intermediary rails. Use the process described above with the template to make the cup holes. The first hole needs to fall approximately 3 in (7.5 cm) above the top of the bottom horizontal support, and holes will then be made every 3 in (7.5 cm) according to the template. Normally you would use three intermediary rails on each wing, spaced evenly, and with no more than a 4 in (10 cm) gap in between to minimise the risk of a horse/pony

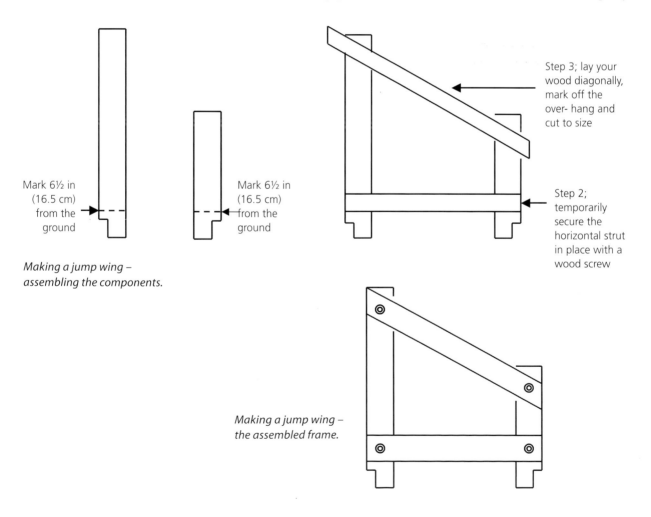

Mark 6½ in (16.5 cm) from the ground

Mark 6½ in (16.5 cm) from the ground

Making a jump wing – assembling the components.

Step 3; lay your wood diagonally, mark off the over- hang and cut to size

Step 2; temporarily secure the horizontal strut in place with a wood screw

Making a jump wing – the assembled frame.

catching its foot. Measure and cut your rails accordingly, and fix with two screws to top and bottom, being careful not to split the wood. The rails can be vertically upright, or can be slightly fanned out to give a more exciting finish. Attach the feet to the wings and you are ready to go.

Making holes for jump cups

This can be a laborious job, so it is generally easier to make a template. Use strong, thick card (you will need to tape a couple of pieces together) and cut it so it is 4 ft long by 4 in wide (1.2 m x 10 cm), which are the dimensions of your jump wing upright.

Measure 1½ in (3.8 cm) in from the edge of the long side and make a mark at the top, bottom and middle.

Next, join these marks and draw a vertical pencil line: this is the line on which the holes will sit.

The holes need to be evenly spaced, with their centres approximately 3 in (7.5 cm) apart.

Starting at the bottom of the template, make a mark every 3 in (7.5 cm) along the pencil line, then use a sharp instrument such as a skewer to poke a hole through over your pencil marks.

These holes give the centre of the holes for your jump cups.

Place the template on the 4 ft (1.2 m) upright of the jump wing and, using a thick marker pen, mark where your holes will need to be drilled.

Drill out the marks on the jump wing, and sand smooth afterwards.

Making a jump wing – the final steps.

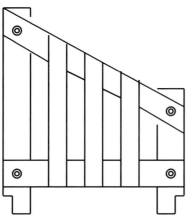

Tip

Treat or paint wood before using it to prolong the life of the jump.

Step 5; make the jump cup holder holes, fix the vertical uprights in place, and lastly attach the jump stand feet

'A' frame jump wings

These wings are not as substantial, sturdy or secure as those described above, however they are cheaper to make, lighter to move and perfectly adequate for schooling exercises. 'A' frame jump wings have only one foot on the front upright. Follow the instructions given earlier (Standard Jump Feet) for making the foot, halving the amount of material needed.

TOOLS YOU WILL NEED

Workbench with clamps
Saw
Sander
Metal ruler
Tri-square
Level
Drill and drill bits
Rubber mallet
Spanner (wrench US)
Tape measure
Pencil

MATERIALS YOU WILL NEED

(NOT INCLUDING THOSE FOR THE FEET, SEE ABOVE)

One 10 ft x 4 in x 2 in (3 m x 10 cm x 5 cm) wooden rail to make the two front
    jump uprights
Two 12 ft x 3 in x 1 in (3.7 m x 7 cm x 2.5 cm) wooden planks to make two
    horizontal supports and the diagonal frame
Appropriate bolts, nuts and washers
About ten 1½ in (38 mm) screws

STEP 1

Take the 10 ft x 4 in (3 m x 10 cm) rail and cut into two lengths of 4 ft (1.2 m) each. These will be the front uprights of the wing. Make the halving joints on the bottom end of each length, as described in Standard Jump Feet. Next, cut the 12 ft x 3 in (3.7m x 7 cm) plank into two 3 ft (91 cm) lengths, which will form the horizontal supports at the bottom of each wing.

STEP 2

Working on one wing at a time, measure ½ in (1.25 cm) above the top of the halving joint channel on the upright and draw a pencil line. Lay the 3 ft

(91 cm) piece with its bottom edge on the pencil line, then take a tri-square and make sure the piece is at an exact right angle with the upright and temporarily secure with two screws.

STEP 3

Using the jump cup hole template, as described earlier (Basic Jump Wing), make your holes in the upright starting 3 in (7.5 cm) above the top of the horizontal support. With the frame lying on the ground, take the 6 ft (1.83 m) piece of 3 in (7.5 cm) plank that was left over from cutting your horizontal supports and position it so that it runs diagonally from the top of the upright to attach to the horizontal support and travel on to be parallel with the bottom of the upright support and the ground. Draw a pencil line at the top end to make the plank flush with the upright and saw off. Next, using a level, draw a pencil line on the bottom end of the diagonal strut, and discard any excess. This will be the part that rests on the ground, effectively the back 'foot', so it needs to be cut absolutely levelly and should be approximately ½ in (1.25 cm) lower than the upright strut – this is to take into account the slight difference in levels caused when the front foot is put on. Temporarily fix the diagonal strut to the top of the upright and to the horizontal support using screws.

STEP 4

Next, double-check that the diagonal support is level to the ground. It can be a good idea at this stage to attach the front foot and stand the wing up. Now you can easily see if your levels and angles are correct, and that the diagonal support is sitting in the right place. Once happy with this, lay the wing back down and drill out one hole at the top to secure the upright and diagonal, and either use a bolt or two screws to secure the horizontal support to the diagonal strut.

STEP 5

Make the jump cup holder holes, fix the vertical uprights in place, and lastly attach the jump stand feet

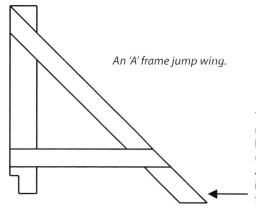

An 'A' frame jump wing.

The diagonal length needs to be slightly longer than the upright to take into account the difference in height when the foot is fixed in place

Fillers

You can be really creative when it comes to jump fillers, provided they are safe for the horse and rider.

Planks

Planks are a popular type of filler, and an alternative to jump poles. They can be made really easily and the decorative aspect can be as fancy as you like and what your painting skills extend to!

TOOLS YOU WILL NEED

Metal rule or preferably a tri-square
Pencil
Saw
Drill (optional)
Screws (optional)

MATERIALS YOU WILL NEED (TO MAKE THREE)

Three 8 ft x 6 in x 1 in (2.4 m x 15 cm x 2.5 cm) treated wooden boards
Twelve 4 x 2 in (10 x 5 cm) metal plates (optional)
Screws (optional)

STEP **1**

Lay your boards flat on the ground (or work bench). Measure 3 in (7.5 cm) in from each end of the boards at the top and bottom and make a mark. Draw a straight vertical line connecting the two marks (use a tri-square if you have one). Next, choose a top end of each plank and measure down the line 2 in (5 cm), make a mark, and then measure 2 in (5 cm) down the plank from the corner, then connect the two marks with a horizontal line.

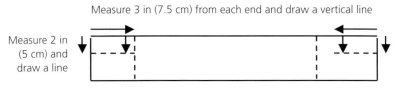

Marking out the plank.

STEP **2**

You now need to carefully saw away following your lines to leave a 3 x 2 in (7.5 x 5 cm) projection at either end of each plank. These will be the pieces that rest on your jump cups.

STEP **3**

These pieces are obviously the weakest point of the structure. If you wish to strengthen them you can attach a pre-drilled metal plate to each side of the projection (see diagram).

Pre-drilled metal plates will strengthen this weak area

Adding metal plates will strengthen the plank.

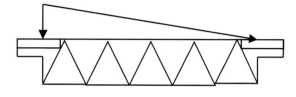

STEP **4**

Your planks are now functional and you can paint them as imaginatively as you wish.

Other ideas for fillers

- Hay or straw bales covered in old dust sheets/bed covers/curtain material. Make sure the material is securely and tightly fastened over the bales.

- Feed bags stuffed with old hay/straw, or other feed bags. Weigh down the bags by placing bricks inside them along their length so they lie horizontally under the jump.

- Using a staple gun, attach the tops of empty feed sacks to your top rail, then pull the sacks tight, slanting them outwards from the bottom of the fence and attach the bottoms of the sacks to a ground pole.

- Fake 'grass' as used for display by greengrocers is excellent if you can track any down. Cover hay/straw bales with it, or attach it to your jump poles as outlined above.

- Old barrels, brightly painted, can be placed underneath the jumps as fillers or used as alternative forms of jump wings.

- Old tyres can be cut in half and placed in a line side by side (see diagram). Fix the tyres laterally to each other with old-fashioned string (this will break in case of accident) and place a rustic pole over them.

- Road cones under a jump make good fillers.

- Improvise a water jump by using a sheet of blue plastic pulled tight and secured between two ground poles. Attach the plastic to the poles with fence staples and position underneath your upright.

Tyre filler jump.

Using car tyres for a fence like this makes a nice small starter jump; try using old machinery tyres, if you can get your hands on them, to make a bigger fence.

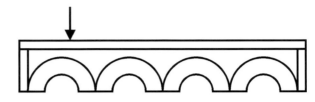

- Old garden benches, if you can come across such a commodity, make excellent fillers of a working hunter type. Place under a rustic upright.

- Old water troughs also make great fillers of cross-country type. However, check for sharp corners or edges and remove any pipe-work, fixtures or fittings.

- Large diameter PVC pipe can be used as an alternative to jump poles, but it can shatter under a direct blow.

If you are creative it is possible to fashion all sorts of jump fillers from bits and pieces lying about the place. However, do be careful not to use anything that might cause injury, and be very aware of sharp edges and corners.

Cavalletti

These are really invaluable as a training aid, for flatwork or for jumping, and once you have become familiar with making one, they are quick and easy to make. Do price-check however, on the cost of your timber and time versus the cost of purchasing. Rustic, unpainted cavalletti can be bought quite cheaply, so make sure you are actually saving money before you embark on your own project. They can be made in 8 ft (2.4 m), 10 ft (3 m) or 12 ft (3.7 m) lengths; the instructions below are for 8 ft (2.4 m) versions.

TOOLS YOU WILL NEED

Saw

Drill, drill bits

Metal ruler

Pencil

Measure

Chisel

Rubber mallet

MATERIALS YOU WILL NEED

Two 8 ft x 4 in x 4 in (2.4 m x 10 cm x 10 cm) squared rails

or:

One 8 ft x 4 in x 4 in (2.4 m x 10 cm x 10 cm) squared rail and one 8 ft x 4 in
  (2.4 m x 10 cm) rounded pole

Two 4 in (10 cm) bolts with washers and nuts

Two 8 in (20 cm) bolts with washers and nuts

STEP **1**

The first step is to make the two X-shaped ends of the cavalletto (which is the singular of 'cavalletti'.) Take the 8 ft (2.4 m) squared rail and cut into four equal 2 ft (61 cm) lengths. Measure and mark the halfway point of each length, making a straight pencil line. Next, measure 2 in (5 cm) on each side of the central line and mark with a pencil line. Turn the pieces of wood over and continue the lines to a depth of 2 in (5 cm). Take a saw and cut through the lines then, using a chisel and rubber mallet, remove the cut section of wood. You should now have four 2 ft (61 cm) pieces of wood, each with a 4 x 2 in (10 x 5 cm) channel cut in them.

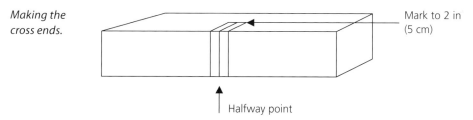

Making the cross ends.

Mark to 2 in (5 cm)

Halfway point

STEP **2**

Slot two pieces together with the cut sides facing each other. You might need to use the mallet to drive them together. Use a measure to find the exact middle, make a mark, then drill a hole through both pieces. Insert your 4 in (10 cm) bolt and secure tightly using a washer and nut. You should now have two free-standing X-structures, which form the two ends of the cavalletto.

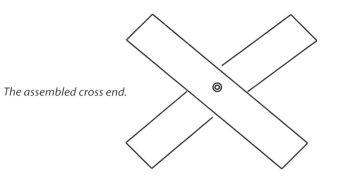

The assembled cross end.

Tip

The directions given here will result in really solidly built cavalletti. You can, if you wish, use a smaller thickness of wood and pole, which will still work, and be cheaper, but will be less durable in the long run.

STEP **3**

Now you need to attach the rail (or pole). Measure 2 in (5 cm) from the end of the rail along its length and draw a line. Next, measure 2 in (5 cm) from the side of the rail in towards your line and make another line: where the two lines intersect should be your centre point, i.e. exactly in the middle of the width of the rail and 2 in (5 cm) in from the end. Drill a hole through the mark, doing the same at the other end of the rail, but making sure to drill the hole on the same side of the rail!

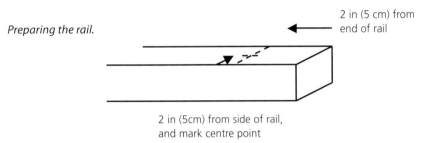

Preparing the rail.

2 in (5 cm) from end of rail

2 in (5cm) from side of rail, and mark centre point

STEP **4**

Set the rail on the X-ends and, taking a pencil, make a mark through your drilled hole and onto the X-end at both ends. Remove the rail and drill a hole on each X-end where your mark is. Replace the rail and drive the 8 in (20 cm) bolts through the holes to secure the rail to the X-ends.

And there you have a homemade cavalletto!

Dressage arenas

Layout of short and long arenas

The short dressage arena is 40 x 20 m (132 x 66 ft) and is marked up as shown in the diagram. (Although imperial equivalents are given, note that dressage arenas are laid out to metric dimensions, and movements carried out within them are always defined in metric terms.) The markers on the centre line are never shown in the actual arena. The quarter markers sit 6 m (20 ft) from the corner, with 14 m (46 ft) between the markers on the long side.

The long dressage arena is 60 x 20 m (196 x 66 ft) and is marked up as shown in the diagram. Again, the markers on the centre line are never shown in the actual arena. As with the short arena there is 6 m (20 ft) between the corner and the quarter markers, but the distances between the other markers on the long sides is 12 m (39 ft), as distinct from 14 m (46 ft) in the short arena.

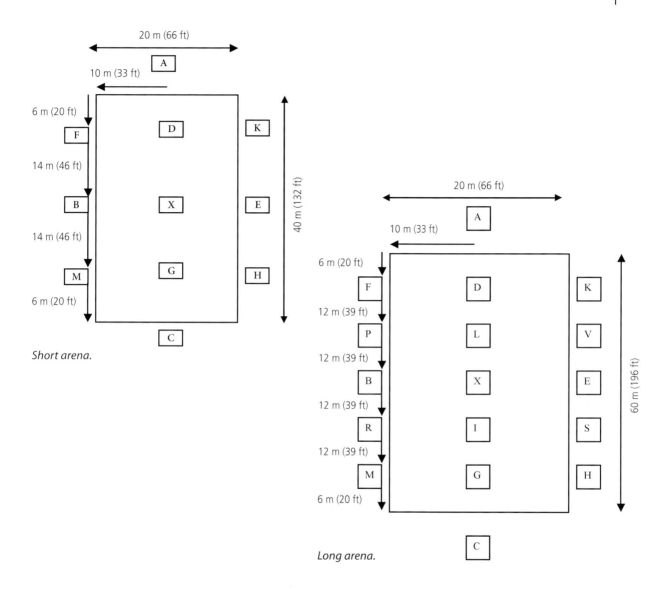

Short arena.

Long arena.

Remembering the sequence of markers

The following useful ditty is good for remembering the order of the perimeter letters in a short arena:

All **K**ing **E**dward's **H**orses **C**an't **M**anage **B**ig **F**ences

And for the centre markers:

All **D**onkeys **X**ing **G**oats **C**arefully

While the following helps with remembering the order of the perimeter letters in a long arena:

All **K**ing **V**ictor **E**dward's **S**how **H**orses **C**anter **M**agnificently **R**ound **B**eautiful **P**rivate **F**arms

And for the centre markers:

All **D**onkeys **L**ove **X**ing **I**rascible **G**oats **C**arefully

Setting out dressage arenas

Actually setting out a dressage arena can be quite tricky, especially getting the arena absolutely rectangular and the corners correct. The easiest way to go about this is first to decide on a flat, level and suitably sized area of paddock, and then mark the first corner with a cone or electric fence post. Measure and mark the second corner, trying to stay as straight as possible – it is much easier to do this with two people. Once all four corners have been roughly marked out at the correct distance you can square the area up by measuring the diagonals from actual corner to corner – i.e. *not* from the quarter markers. This measurement and line is the key element in achieving square corners. The diagonal line for a short arena must measure 44.72 m (146 ft 8 in), and for a long arena 63.24 m (207 ft 6 in) in order for the corners and distances to be correct.

Ideas for makeshift marker letters

Paint letters onto suitably large, stable, safe objects:

- Road cones with the letters painted on them work very well for making markers.

- Large milk jugs also work well. Fill the jugs with water or sand and paint the letters on the side.

- Letters can also be painted onto old barrels or buckets (large supplement buckets are particularly good), but remove the handles to prevent injury.

- If you have access to old bits of wood (broken planks work well) then cut them to size, paint the letters on, nail a stake to the back and drive into the ground. Make sure the top of the stake is flush with the top of the marker to minimise the risk of injury.

- You can also make your own markers by hinging together two pieces of wood, approximately 10 x 10 in (26 x 26 cm) at the top and painting the letters on. Hinged markers like this are useful because they fold flat and are easy to store.

- For an indoor arena letters can be printed off a computer, laminated and pinned to the wall.

Ideas for marking out the arena edge

- One of the easiest ways to mark out a makeshift arena in a field is to simply mow the outside track, bearing in mind that it might need to be repeated periodically as the grass grows. If the area is mown it can also be helpful to spray-paint a single line marking the exterior perimeter, but you will need a steady hand!

- If mowing your perimeter lines it can be helpful to mow the centre line, but make sure you get it straight.

- Use old show jumping poles, but make sure they remain straight and don't get kicked out of line.

- Large diameter PVC pipe makes excellent arena edging and is relatively inexpensive to purchase. (As suggested earlier, it can also be used for trotting or jumping poles.)

- Cones used as the letter markers also clearly delineate the arena area.

- Barrels also work well, and can again be used for the letter markers (as well as for show jump wings and fillers).

- You can make your own edging by painting planks white and fixing short lengths off wood on the backs (see diagram) to allow them to be propped up. Ideally, they should slant away from the track slightly. However, before embarking on this project check the price of wood against the cost of buying ready-made edging to make sure you are not going to be out of pocket.

- For added effect, place a flower tub on either side of the entrance to the arena at A. (Don't use poisonous plants, and don't leave tubs out if the horse has access unsupervised access to them!)

Make sure that whatever edging you use is safe, and with this in mind avoid stakes (unless specific for the job), wire, tape or chain. If you wish to use white chain for a competition arena you must use the plastic variety that will snap and break should a horse catch its leg.

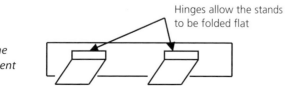

Hinges allow the stands to be folded flat

Arena edging seen from the back to show the attachment of the supports.

APPENDIX

Making horse treats

Most horses have to make do with the occasional mint, sugar lump or carrot, but for the truly dedicated horse lover the following recipes for treats make an enjoyable alternative – at least for the horse! Most of these recipes are variations of a similar theme. Provided you use any combination of carrot, apple, oats, treacle and flour you can hardly go wrong.

The reluctant chef treat

INGREDIENTS

¾ pint (0.43 litre) unsweetened applesauce
8 oz (225 grams) oat bran cereal or ground oatmeal
4 oz (114 grams) plain flour

STEP 1
Preheat the oven to 350ºF (180ºC) and grease a 9 x 9 in (23 x 23 cm) square baking tray.

STEP 2
Mix the ingredients together and spread evenly in the tray. Bake for approximately 25 minutes or until the mixture starts to shrink away from the edges of the tray, and hardens.

STEP 3
Slice into pieces while still warm, then allow to cool and keep in an airtight container in the fridge.

Tip

Keep treats in an airtight container to prolong their life, write the date they were made on the lid and, dependent on the ingredients, use within two weeks.

Quick and easy treats

INGREDIENTS

Four grated carrots
One finely chopped apple
8 oz (225 grams) rolled oats
8 oz (225 grams) plain flour
2 tbsp corn oil
4 tbsp molasses or treacle or golden syrup
1 tsp salt

STEP 1

Preheat oven to 350ºF (180ºC) and grease a medium-sized baking tray (the smaller the tray, the thicker the treats).

STEP 2

Mix all the ingredients together in a large bowl and spread evenly into the tray. It can be helpful to score the mixture at this point.

STEP 3

Cook for 20 minutes or until golden brown. Cut the treats and allow to cool. Keep refrigerated, but try to remember to take them out of the fridge for an hour or so before feeding them.

Clear round carrot cake

INGREDIENTS

Three grated or shredded carrots
One finely chopped apple
6 oz (170 grams) bran
6 oz (170 grams) oats (rolled, crushed or oatmeal)
6 oz (170 grams) plain flour
4 oz (114 grams) brown sugar
5 tbsp molasses or treacle or golden syrup
4 fl oz (120 ml) water

STEP 1

Preheat oven to 400ºF (205ºC) and grease a muffin tin or Yorkshire pudding tray.

STEP 2

Mix all the ingredients, keeping a little of the brown sugar to one side. Pour the doughy mixture into the tin/tray and sprinkle the remaining brown sugar on top.

STEP 3

Bake for approximately 30 minutes, cool and refrigerate.

Apple delight

INGREDIENTS

Two sliced apples

8 oz (225 grams) rolled or crushed oats, or oatmeal

8 oz (225 grams) brown sugar

2 tbsp margarine or cooking butter

STEP 1

Melt the butter in a saucepan over a moderate heat, then add the sugar and stir until the mixture comes to the boil. Turn down the heat and simmer for 5 minutes.

STEP 2

Dip the apple slices in the sugar mixture until they are well covered, then coat with the oats.

STEP 3

Place them on a wire rack on one side until they have cooled.

Minty twists

INGREDIENTS

Ten crushed peppermints (Polo mints or Lifesavers are very good)

Two diced apples

8 oz (225 grams) rolled or crushed oats, or oatmeal

8 oz (225 grams) plain flour

4 tbsp molasses or treacle or golden syrup

STEP 1

Preheat oven to 180ºC (350ºF) and grease a medium-sized baking tray.

STEP **2**

Mix the flour, oats and molasses together and gradually add a little water until the mixture is doughy. Stir in the peppermints and apple.

STEP **3**

Bake in the oven for about 20 minutes, or until they turn golden brown.

Gallop-on gourmets

INGREDIENTS

Two finely chopped apples

24 oz (680 grams) oats, rolled, crushed or oatmeal

4 tbsp molasses or treacle or golden syrup or honey

1 pint (0.57 litre) water

3 tbsp plain flour

2 tbsp brown sugar

4 oz (114 grams) raisins

STEP **1**

Preheat the oven to 375°F (190°C) and grease a muffin tin or Yorkshire pudding tray.

STEP **2**

Mix together the oats, water and molasses and warm over a moderate heat, then add the apple, sugar, flour and raisins, and continue to heat the mixture through, stirring constantly.

STEP **3**

Pour the mixture into the tin/tray and bake for approximately 20 minutes, or until golden brown.

Stable sweets

INGREDIENTS

One finely chopped carrot

8 oz (225 grams) rolled oats

4 tbsp sweet feed mix, or crushed horse and pony nuts

4 tbsp water

2 tbsp honey

2 tbsp smooth peanut butter

STEP 1
Mix the oats and the water in a bowl and add the honey and peanut butter. Stir well and add the sweet feed mix and chopped carrot. If the mixture is not sticking together add more honey or molasses.

STEP 2
Roll the mixture into small balls, set on a wire tray and place in the fridge to harden.

Dressage diva pick-me-ups

INGREDIENTS
One apple finely chopped
One carrot finely chopped
8 oz (225 grams) oatmeal
4 tbsp honey
4 oz (114 grams) plain flour
Some milk

STEP 1
Preheat the oven to 350ºF (180ºC) and grease a flat baking tray.

STEP 2
Mix all the ingredients together well in a large bowl and add a little milk until the mixture becomes doughy.

STEP 3
Roll the mixture into ball-shaped treats and bake for 20 minutes, or until golden brown. Allow to cool, and keep refrigerated.

Final furlong biscuits

INGREDIENTS
One grated carrot
One grated apple
4 oz (114 grams) bran
4 oz (114 grams) oats, rolled or crushed or oatmeal
12 oz (340 grams) plain flour
8 oz (225 grams) molasses or treacle or golden syrup or honey
A little sugar and a glass

STEP **1**

Preheat oven to 375°F (190°C) and lightly grease two baking sheets/trays.

STEP **2**

Combine the ingredients in a large bowl and mix together well. It should be a sticky, doughy consistency. Drop the mixture in small balls onto the baking sheets, then grease the bottom of the glass, dip it in the sugar and press down on each ball to flatten them out.

STEP **3**

Bake for approximately 10 minutes or until golden brown, allow to cool and store in an airtight container in the fridge.

Index